ROAM WITH ME

A MEMOIR

ROAM WITH ME

Finding the Extraordinary in the Ordinary

BONNI CHALKIN

Verybonni Press

NEW YORK

Without limitation, nothing contained in this book should replace medical advice, medical visits, or recommendations from health care providers. Patients should always consult with a doctor or other health care provider for medical advice.

Versions of both sections of "No Small Change" previously appeared as "An Unforgettable Act of Sharing" and "I Know You Exist" in *Re-Creating Our Common Cord: A Wising Up Anthology* (Wising Up Press, October 2019), *Goodness: A Wising Up Anthology* (Wising Up Press, 2020), and *And Then* (Vol. 20, 2019). A version of "The Road Behind the Road" previously appeared as "A Breath in Time" in *The Power of the Pause: The Wonder of Our Here & Now* (Wising Up Press, 2022) and *And Then* (Vol. 22, 2024).

Some names of individuals have been changed to protect their privacy.

Book design by Timothy Shaner, NightandDayDesign.biz

ISBN: 979-8-218-47207-8 (Paperback)

ISBN: 979-8-218-47208-5 (e-book)

Verybonni.com

And the universe said,

"Come where the ordinary becomes extraordinary.

Come roam with me." And so I did.

· CONTENTS ·

CONTENTS

CONTENTS

PART VII: CONNECTED

PART VIII: NO RUSH

ROAM WITH ME

PREFACE

It took me years to finally jump in and put all these stories together. As I wrote them, each one came alive inside me, and I was reminded over and over how these tales are so much bigger than I am. Most things are.

A little background before we dive into these short scenes from my life: I grew up in the small town of Jericho on Long Island, New York. Since I was a little girl, I have always felt attuned to the world in an unusual way. I often have unique experiences meeting incredible people at just the right time, sharing deep conversations with strangers, and being amazed by the synchronicities that abound.

I married three times—a long-running show I playfully call "My Three Husbands." My second husband, who is the father of my two children, Montana and London, is the well-known actor Judd Hirsch. Yes, he's in some stories here, as are the other two, along with some pre- and between-marriage love interests.

I graduated from Boston University, where I met husband number one; went on to work in fashion design and sales for a women's clothing company in New York City's Garment District; and eventually embraced my intuitive abilities to become an energy healer.

My stories venture through personal experiences such as overcoming a debilitating illness, an eating disorder, and a learning disability, and many involve supernatural occurrences, from psychic visions and instantaneous manifestations to out-of-body events and clues about past lives. My reflections also center on kindness, gratitude, tolerance, being open to signs from the universe, and how a stranger can change the course of your life in an instant.

My decision to finally break through my lifelong doubts about my writing skills—and reluctance to focus on myself in this way—sprang from an early memory.

One day when I was five years old, I was at Atlantic Beach with my *Nanny*, my grandmother. She took my hand and led me down to the water's edge. I kept dipping my toes in and then scrambling back onto the sand. "Why don't you go in all the way?" Nanny asked after watching this play out a few times.

"It's too cold!"

She picked me up in her arms and gently tossed me into the water. I was startled at first, but the water quickly became warm as I splashed about, playing and laughing. I was having so much fun it took her some time to get me out of the ocean to go have lunch. When I finally rose from the water, she took my hand, bent down to look me in the eyes, and said, "Bonni, you'll never truly know what something is unless you jump in all the way."

Learning how to leap ultimately pushed me to produce this memoir, a gathering of memorable moments that impacted me and others. Those moments made me who I am today.

Thank you for joining me.

PART I

LEARNING THE ROPES

If you plant yourself in fertile soil,

you can't help but bloom.

We are all beings with limitless possibilities,

so love deeply, have adventures, and take risks.

LESSONS IN WRITING

The email subject line read, "Come Experience a Teacher Night." They invited parents of students, alumni, and even parents of alumni (that's me) to attend and experience what a high school class was like at the Dalton School. My daughter, Montana, and her best friend, Danielle (also known as my other daughter), had graduated from the school on New York City's Upper East Side eleven years earlier.

Curious, I opened the email (which could have easily gone unseen because I usually forget to scroll down beyond what's right in my face). I thought I'd just read through the list of classes and delete. But when I came across Creative Writing, my heart skipped a beat. I signed up immediately and paid the twenty dollars. The night finally arrived. Walking through the Dalton doors, I felt a sense of nostalgia. The familiar main-floor lobby, subtle scent of polished floors, and students' mind-blowing artwork lining the walls swept me back to when the kids were young.

I planned to skip the six o'clock cocktail hour, but when I arrived a bit early, I changed my mind. The room was packed with parents and alumni. I knew none of them. When I finished my quick walk through the large room laden with tables of crackers and cheese and wine, I skipped down the steps to room 205. I was the first to arrive and immediately felt intimidated. My old insecurities blew up inside me like forced air pumped into a balloon about to pop. As a kid, having dyslexia before it was a known condition made life difficult, to say the least. My years of doing poorly in school planted seeds of doubt in my mind, now ridden with overgrown weeds.

I saw a woman with short brown hair seated at the far end of an oval table near the window. She was to be our teacher that night. Her smile and friendliness made me more comfortable, but not enough to give up my old childhood ways. I took a seat at the opposite end of the table, as far away from her as possible, as I had always done when I was a student. The table filled up fast.

She had us all say our names and tell the group a little bit about ourselves and our child's name, and, if we could, name a recent book we loved reading and why. We went around the room. The last person to speak was a young woman who was in the business management industry. She had a seven-year-old at Little Dalton and a four-year-old at home. She mentioned a recent best-seller she was reading that she loved, but I didn't catch the title because I'm a little hard of hearing. I only heard this: "And you know what's so cool? It was this author, Bonnie's, first book and she wrote it in her sixties!" I thought I was hearing things. "Did you say Bonnie?" I asked. "*Bonnie?*" She said yes. Overwhelmed with joy, flinging my arms in the air, I blurted out to the class, "My name is Bonni, and I'm in my sixties and writing my first book! A memoir!"

I took it as a sign from the universe.

Then Loryn, our teacher, gave us a few writing exercises with prompts. She invited us to share our work, but it wasn't mandatory. We were all totally engaged. Loryn had that way about her—kind, calm, and inspiring at the same time. I loved her energy. She was a wonderful teacher who had become the director of the high school at the Dalton School. She must miss teaching, I thought; she's so good at it. I read aloud two of the four short pieces I wrote that night. The first wasn't very good, most likely because I took my own words from something I had already written and tried to incorporate it into the exercise (was that cheating?). I was nervous and couldn't shake my fear of writing on command. One woman, though, commented that she liked a line from my piece. Phew.

For our last exercise, Loryn gave us a word and told us to write whatever came to mind from that word. She repeated the exercise three more times. I decided just to let go of my fear and do as she said. Her second word was "Tupperware." Hmm. *Tupperware.* So, I wrote:

It was hard and strong, useful and full.
I emptied it, only to refill it
With the failures and successes of the very next day.

I chose to take another risk and read it out loud. After I finished, Loryn excitedly pointed at me and spoke across the table, "Now *this* should go in your memoir!"
She liked it. My teacher liked it!
That was a first.

We heal our past by moving forward.

BE LIKE THE BUFFALO

There was a time I experienced a very painful chapter of my life. I was a mother with two small children: a nine-year-old and a two-year-old. I was going through a difficult divorce from my second husband, the actor Judd Hirsch. Although ending our marriage was mutual, breaking up a family is always devastating to everyone involved.

At the same time, I lost one of my closest friends and endured nine other deaths as well. One was a neighbor, another my uncle Sam (an uncle by heart, not by blood), and some were our beloved pets: bunnies, two goats, a degu, and my favorite dog, a rescue named Lucius. I had lived with him longer than anyone.

While going through this extremely tough time, I remembered the words given to me by a wise, mysterious older woman I had met many years earlier. "Be like the buffalo," she said. I learned later that buffalo symbolize bravery, kindness, strength, and manifesting our desires. She meant all that and something else as well. She continued, "When a storm is approaching, most animals seek shelter or run away. But the buffalo, they do the complete opposite. They head right into the storm."

At first, I didn't get it. I was already in the storm; all I wanted to do was run away from it. Day after day, I lay in bed. I didn't move. I allowed the pain to consume me.

I was caught in the perfect storm: death, divorce, and moving. Then it hit me. By heading directly into the storm, the buffalo faces the most intense parts right away and gets through it much faster. I needed to face my obstacles, not avoid them.

We are wired to be on the alert and wary of the unknown as a matter of survival, but we are not prisoners of that wiring. The wise woman's words I remembered that day gave me the strength to get out of bed and keep going. I didn't know it then, but I was undergoing a life-altering transformation.

Once I decided to step into that storm and face the many challenges and changes before me, a new and wondrous world emerged. Feeling the sadness, fear, and anger, those energies were brought to the surface and released, propelling me to the other side. It's not always easy, but I try to remind myself with each and every storm that I, too, have the strength and courage, just like the buffalo, to keep going forward one step at a time.

It takes only one drop to start

filling the deepest well.

MY FATHER'S GIFT

When I was eight years old, my mom, dad, older sister, and I were driving home to Long Island after visiting my grandparents in Manhattan. They lived in the cool section of the city, Greenwich Village, where in the 1960s, hippies hung out and music played all day and night in Washington Square Park. My grandparents lived on Fifth Avenue right across from the park, and I loved going out on their terrace, which had a perfect view of the big stone arch and all the people gathering and making music below. Our occasional visits to our grandparents also came with a stroll to the unique stores on nearby 8th Street, where each of us kids got a new pair of shoes and, to top it off, a fresh-squeezed, frothy Orange Julius.

On that trip home when I was eight, my father said he wanted to show us girls something. Instead of taking our usual route through the Midtown Tunnel, he kept driving north all the way beyond the top of Central Park into Harlem. He explained that he wanted us to know how other people lived outside our grandparents' neighborhood and our small town on Long Island. As we slowly rode past broken-down buildings that hot summer day, I asked my dad what they were, and he said they were homes where people lived. In front of one building, children were trying to cool off in the spray of a broken fire hydrant. My father explained that these people didn't have enough money to live in a house like we did. The little kids playing in the water seemed happy, but I was worried about their bare feet on the bits of junk and broken glass that shined on the sidewalk. I felt sad for them. I thought everybody had what we had. I didn't understand. Why didn't everyone have . . . enough?

That evening, we went to one of my favorite childhood restaurants, The Jolly Fisherman. Dinner there was always a special treat with their great seafood and french fries, and most times, I got the lobster. When it came to my turn to order, my father asked me what I wanted to eat.

"Nothing," I said.

"Why?" he asked. "Aren't you feeling well?"

I started to cry and said, "I don't want to live in the street."

In my eight-year-old mind, I didn't want my dad to buy me dinner with money he should save to keep us from losing our house. He ordered me something anyway, but I was too upset to eat and sat quietly through the meal. When I went to bed that night, pictures from the day flowed through my mind: dirty brick buildings, broken windows, block after block of cement instead of grass, and barefoot children in torn clothes. And there I was, tucked in my nice soft bed in my pretty lavender painted room, with clothes hanging in the closet and shoes lined up beneath them. That was the night my well of gratitude began to fill up.

All these years later, I am still grateful to my father for offering this experience to me as a child, unlike Siddhartha's father in Hermann Hesse's novel, who was set on sheltering his son from the world's pain and only reluctantly gave in after Siddhartha had already snuck out of the palace and saw how others lived for the first time. My father made a point of showing me the world, a different world just a few miles away from mine. And that experience had a profound effect on me as a little girl.

My father understood the importance of seeing the world's pain in order to grow, and that made all the difference. For me, growth means becoming more aware, empathetic, and compassionate and finding ways to lessen suffering. Even the smallest distress is a suffering worth attending to with any act of kindness. When I do, I feel more myself.

I have my father to thank for that.

Tolerance is creating harmony with

those who are different.

THE BOY IN THE HAT

Before I got married and had children, I spent a year in Montana working at an outdoor residential treatment center, which also included a wilderness therapy program for teens and young men ages fourteen to twenty-four.

They say you teach what you most need to learn. At the time, I was a cigarette smoker, so in my own way, I knew about addiction. The center focused on cognitive behavioral therapy, which helped these boys understand the thoughts and emotions that fed their addictions. In addition, they also showed the boys healthier and more productive ways to understand and express themselves. The treatment center also incorporated the Twelve-Step Program, which fosters recovery by guiding individuals through a process of spiritual reflection, acceptance, and support.

My job was to intern for the wilderness part of the program, but I had the same responsibilities as the other counselors when we went on a two- or three-week wilderness trip. These trips were about self-discovery to help the boys gain confidence, awareness, humility, and the endurance needed to conquer their addictions.

On one of the trips, we were in the middle of the beautiful, majestic Glacier National Park. The first evening, after a long day of hiking and mountain climbing, we were all sitting around a warm fire reading from *Day by Day*, a book of daily meditations for alcoholics and addicts. At least that's what it was called then. That night, the daily meditation asked us to give up something we loved to another person. I chose to go first.

I knew that Mick, a sixteen-year-old boy, really liked my hat. He would constantly ask to try it on and told me many times how much he liked it, how much he wanted one. I acquired the red baseball-style hat with "Voyageur Outward Bound" embossed in white letters after my own three-week adventure hiking and canoeing in the breathtaking Boundary Waters of northern Minnesota. That hat meant a lot to me. It was a constant reminder of all I had achieved there.

I slowly removed my prized hat from my head and handed it to Mick. The shocked look he gave me was priceless. I don't think I'll ever forget it. Although it was customary in these types of programs for all of us to hug a lot, that night, along with so many thank-yous, I got an extra-long hug from Mick. What happened the very next day still burns in my memory.

We were preparing for the day's hike, leaving our tents behind and only taking a pack filled with food, water, and other sundries. Standing somewhat near Mick and Adam, I could hear their conversation while dismantling my one-person Eureka tent. Adam lived on the Blackfoot Reservation in northwest Montana, while Mick was from a small town out West. These were the two I had become closest to, and they were complete opposites. Adam stood about five feet eight inches tall and had a strong build and long, silky black hair. Mick was tall and quite thin, with pale skin. Their personalities were foreign to each other as well—Adam was laid-back and quiet, while Mick was hyper and boisterous. Even so, they had become good friends.

Mick had run out of his M&M's and I heard him ask Adam if he could have some of his. Adam said, "No. You ate all of yours and I've been rationing and only have a few left." Mick turned to him and said nastily, "Quit being a Jew." Now, it was my turn to be shocked.

I couldn't believe the words that just flew out of Mick's mouth, the very boy I had given my precious hat to the night before. I did a quick pirouette and sprinted to where the boys were standing. I faced them both and stared into Mick's eyes. Calmly, I said, "Mick, I'm Jewish."

He was utterly shocked. "What?"

I repeated myself, "I'm Jewish."

Mick stood frozen. Shell shocked. He took a moment to collect himself and, after regaining his sixteen-year-old composure, expressed how sorry he was. I could tell he really meant it, and not just because the two of us had become close. He had tears in his eyes when he said it. He told me he'd never known anyone who was Jewish but heard his parents talk like that all the time. He kept apologizing. I told him I forgave him but he didn't want to let it go, saying that he would never ever speak like that again and would not accept it if anyone else did.

Mission accomplished.

I don't know many people who can turn themselves around that quickly, especially about something as stitched-in as their biases. That's who Mick was at sixteen. I have a feeling he's grown into an even better man today.

A mentor can appear in many disguises.

I'M MORE THAN JUST A GIRL

While working at the boys and young men treatment center in northwest Montana, I went on our second two-week winter trip with the guys in Glacier National Park and the Bob Marshall Wilderness. We had to bushwhack through the snow on cross-country skis through the backcountry—no trail, no nothing. The snow skis were shorter and wider than most, which served me well as I'm only five feet three inches. This made it easier since we also had to carry a heavy backpack stuffed with all our needs for the trek.

I'll never forget two experiences from that trip. First, a therapy counselor had broken one of his poles, so I, being an intern and not a counselor or wilderness leader, was asked to give up one of mine. Since I was told you can't ski with one pole, I was also told I was to stay back at camp all day. Alone. My job was to make sure dinner was prepared and ready to eat when they all got back a little before the sun went down, around 4:30 p.m. Mountain time. I was raving mad, assuming it was because I was the only female on a trip with fourteen males.

Growing up as a suburban Long Islander and city girl in the Big Apple, I was completely unequipped to be left alone in the wild. It was all foreign to me, especially the snowy wilderness with the frigid temperatures. Since we bushwhacked in, there were no trails. At first, my mind raced with, "What if I get hurt? What if they never come back, and I'm stuck here without knowing how to get out? I could freeze to death, starve to death." I thought about the day before when we were going over a ridge, and the wind was so strong that it knocked me over. My backpack was so heavy it was hard to get up on my own, so I was grateful that one of the boys, Adam, helped me.

I went through all the bad scenarios I thought could happen. After finally running out of all the disasters I could fathom, the best thing I could think of doing in those days before meditation was popular was some deep breathing. Why not? I had read an article about breathwork and fig- ured it couldn't hurt. I became still. *Accept what's happening.* Okay, I'll sit in my newly acquired Crazy Creek chair in the winter sun and read my book.

At several points throughout the day, I took a moment to marvel at the serene, sparkling white scenery before me. I began to enjoy my solitude as I became one with my surroundings. I don't recall all the details, the empty spaces between the memorable moments, but it doesn't matter. Nature itself taught me a great lesson: the miraculous begins within oneself.

The day went faster than I anticipated. Even still, I had such a sense of relief when I heard familiar voices in the distance. That night, I made a spicy mac and cheese with some cayenne pepper over the ever-reliable Coleman stoves. The cayenne gave it a kick and kept us warm when the temperature dropped well below freezing. Everyone enjoyed the meal. I learned something about myself during those long hours alone that afternoon, but it didn't compare to the difficult lesson I was about to learn the next day.

The program founder, Jack B., met us early the next morning, about six days into the trip when we were all to go to his "super cool lodge" for an overnight counselor meeting. I was excited to start the day's adventure since I had heard that the lodge was rustic yet very picturesque and cozy. Truly one of a kind.

Because I had signed up to intern for the program for only a year, I was overjoyed to know I would experience the place. Not everyone who worked there had the same privilege. Some had worked in the program for years and were never invited. You couldn't drive to the lodge. You could only hike in during the warmer summer months or ski in during the winter months.

My excitement led to a burst of energy that morning. There I was, happily gliding along on my backcountry skis while the hours flew by. As the sun started to descend, Jack B. came over to me. "Okay, Bonni, it's your turn to pull one of the sleds." At first, I thought I misunderstood him. Each sled was packed solid with food and equipment needed for the entire wilderness trip.

"What?"

He repeated, "It's your turn to pull one of the sleds."

I am a small-framed woman and, at the time, weighed maybe 110 pounds at most. I was strong back then, but not that strong. I panicked and stood frozen as he strapped the heavy sled to my body. I didn't know how I would find my way to the lodge. I knew I wouldn't be able to keep up with the group pulling that kind of weight.

He told me to go straight, follow the stream, listen for their voices, and make sure the sun was always to my left. That would take me right to the lodge. I thought, *What sun? The sun is going down!*

"You'll be fine," he said, and they all left. I started crying.

Through my tears, I started mumbling aloud, "I'm just a girl in my late twenties from *New York City* who doesn't know how to *do* this!" I thought I was going to die out there. Then I became angry—very angry. That anger pushed me forward, forcing me to move. I went slowly, as the sled's massive weight created a sense that we were two opposing forces at work. After what seemed like an eternity, by some miracle, I saw distant lights radiating through the darkness.

Shortly afterward, I found myself standing in front of the lodge. Everyone—the kids, counselors, wilderness guides, and, of course, Jack B.—had already eaten dinner and were all warmed up and joyfully gathered around the giant fireplace. They told me they'd saved me some food that had been prepared on the wood-burning cooking stove in the kitchen and gestured for me to go help myself. I was furious but couldn't help admiring the unique, warm surroundings. The place was beautiful. I was starving and gulped down my dinner.

When I finished, I went straight into the Great Room, where Jack B. sat alone on the couch. I couldn't wait to give him a piece of my mind. Owner or not, at that moment, I couldn't care less who he was or whether I got kicked out of the program. I noticed another counselor standing nearby. I didn't care if there was an audience either. As I saw it, Jack B. had left me out in the woods to die.

I stomped over to the couch, glared down at him, and yelled, "Do you know I could have died out there? I had no idea what I was doing or where I was going. How could you do such a thing? Who do you think you are? You're such a chauvinist. I know you hate women!" I went on and on. I can't remember what else I screamed in my incensed state.

When I finally stopped my tirade, he calmly looked up from the couch and stared at me. "I did it for you, Bonni." I looked at him like he was crazy. "What!?" He continued, "I did it for you, to show you are so much more capable than you think you are." He paused to let that sink in. "I saw in you what you are capable of, Bonni. I also knew you didn't see that in yourself."

For once, I was speechless. He was right. I burst into tears.

This man, who was basically a stranger, thought enough of me to help me, even though I wasn't one of his clients but just an intern. Those twelve months I'd spent there, constantly being challenged, had already become intensely meaningful to me, but nothing compared to the lesson Jack B. taught me that night—that I was actually a capable person. My life took a turn in that dusky, woodfire-scented old room, and I will always be grateful.

True masters follow their own footsteps.

NO TROUBLE READING

When I was a little girl in elementary school, my teachers noticed I had trouble reading. I was really slow. I just couldn't catch on . . . or catch up. The trouble followed me through junior high school and beyond. I was placed in the C reading group, the lowest. None of my friends were there because they were in the A group. I remember how bad it made me feel; I felt like an outcast. To make matters worse, my parents, through no fault of their own, would talk about this when I was out of the room, thinking I couldn't hear them. They'd say things like, "No, Bonni can't go to Hebrew school. She can't join the gymnastics club—she has enough trouble reading and getting her homework done." They were always completely unaware that I'd been eavesdropping. I'd hide out of sight and hear every harsh word. I thought they thought I was stupid. I thought I was stupid.

The only subject I was able to excel in was math. It made sense to me. I loved numbers. Letters were a different story. I couldn't spell; I interchanged letters; it was hard to follow directions; my word order was sometimes different from others (a backward little); and reading was almost impossible. Much later the root of my problems in school was finally revealed like hidden thorns that had been scratching at my skin for years. I had dyslexia. The thorns still hurt, but at least I knew what was wrong with me.

My senior year in high school was life-changing. Our English teacher gave us a book to read about an Englishman who got lost in the African Congo and eventually became the leader of a local tribe. I can't remember the details or name of the book, or even my teacher's name, for that matter. What I do remember is that when I started reading the book, the usual anticipated dread disappeared like dew on a blade of grass kissed by the morning sun. Even today, I wish I could recall the title so I could read it again. It was the first large novel I ever attempted and read to completion. That was my very first step up the steep stairway to finally being able to enjoy reading.

Eventually, I went to college. Yes, shockingly, I got accepted into Boston University (it was the only acceptance I got, but hey, I met husband number-one there!). I was accepted to the College of Basic Studies program. That's what the special program that accepted students who didn't do very well in high school or on the SATs was called back then. It was a two-year program that, upon completion, integrated us "outcasts" into the regular BU undergrad school for our junior and senior years.

I felt pretty insecure about my reading and spelling skills. English was, after all, my worst subject. Computers weren't around then, so my roommates became my "go-to" spell-check. I always had to ask them for help whenever a paper was due. I remember feeling stressed and inferior because my grades were so much lower than those of my *smart* new college friends.

During those summers home from college, though, my love affair with books, with reading, started. The first book I stumbled upon that summer was titled *Lady* by Thomas Tryon. It takes place in a fictional small town in New England. The story is about a young boy's preoccupation and friendship with his neighbor, a mysterious widow. I want to read *Lady* again and wonder if it will have the same effect on me after all these years. I was totally taken by it. It was hauntingly beautiful, with a surprise twist ending that shook me. The title stayed with me all these years like a favorite, worn sweater I won't leave behind. I continued to tackle books one by one. I realized that the more I read, the faster I read. Well, let's not get carried away—faster for me, that is, but I am still slow compared to the masses. I managed to develop a passion for reading regardless. Instead of a chore, reading became a joy.

I always had a vivid imagination, and I remember my mom constantly, yet lovingly, telling me to get my head out of the clouds. It was that imagination that helped me develop a passion for writing. Many years later, my writings were published. That little girl who struggled so much in school would have never believed she would one day become a writer. Shadows appear to remind us we're standing in the light. It taught me a wonderful lesson. Never allow anyone—including ourselves—to place limits on us.

I was always told I can't.

I learned . . . I can.

Self-discovery is the light that shines

from within to help us heal from trauma.

HIDING PLACES

No one could find him.

Howie and I were six years old when we played hide-and-seek that late afternoon on that warm, sunshine-filled day. Usually, about five or six kids from our block met outside to play. That day, eight of us showed up for a game of hide-and-seek. Howie and his two older brothers lived across the street from me in a white split-level home with black window trims, while Johnny and Joey lived in the red brick ranch house next to his, diagonally across from mine. My mom, Audrey, and Howie's mom, Barbara (I called her Aunt Barbara), were best friends. They didn't socialize much with Johnny and Joey's mom or dad, whose names I don't remember. I do remember Johnny and Joey's house, though: they had a wide wooden plank leading up to their front door instead of stairs because their father was in a wheelchair. I never found out why he couldn't walk or what had happened to him. Their father frightened me because he never smiled or said hello. He just stared. Joey, the younger brother, was emotionally challenged, and Johnny, as I recall, was really cute. He had dark hair, a Beatles haircut, and big brown eyes. He was the quiet older brother I secretly had a crush on. Oh, summer! Such fun times as we all played together and loved being outside when the weather was warm and the sky stayed lit.

That late afternoon, it was Howie's older brother Gary's turn to be the seeker. Gary had a dominating personality and was the leader of the group. Since Howie and I were the youngest, we always hid together. When Gary covered his eyes, leaned his face against a tree, and started counting, Howie grabbed my hand and said, "Let's go." He led me around to the back of his white split-level home and pointed to an alcove that was partially hidden by their new brick barbeque. We ducked in there and stayed put for what seemed like hours. No one came. I was sure we had won. I was excited because we had never won before.

It was starting to get dark when I finally heard my mother yell, "Bonni, come in! It's time for dinner!" I left my perfect hiding spot with pride and went across the street to my house, pretended to wash my hands at the sink, and sat down at the dinner table. As we started eating our tuna casserole, one of my favorite meals, we heard frantic knocking at our door. We all ran to see who it was. There stood Aunt

Barbara, hollering, "They can't find John! They can't find John!" The grownups called Johnny, "John." My parents left the house and told me and my older sister, Sharon, to stay home as they combed the neighborhood looking for Johnny. Even the local fire department came to help with the search after the adults concluded he was nowhere to be found.

I remember feeling so scared. It had already been dark for a couple of hours when my mom and dad finally returned. My mom had tears in her eyes. "They found Johnny," she said softly. "He's dead." She went on, "He must have tried to climb into his window and grabbed onto the flower box, which was hidden by the tall bushes in the front of his house, and it fell on his head, killing him." He was ten. I was devastated. I also thought it was my fault. I never told anyone, but I thought if I hadn't stayed in our hiding spot so long, maybe they would have found him sooner and saved him. At six years old, I felt completely responsible for Johnny's accidental death. His family, so distraught, put their house up for sale and moved away shortly after.

I was traumatized by Johnny's death and the belief that I thought I alone was responsible. No one explained anything to me, maybe because I was only six. No one talked about it at all after that dark, tragic night. I kept all my feelings a secret, buried deep inside, but they came out in other ways. I developed a nervous twitch in my right eye. My family thought I had a brain tumor, so they sent me to a neurologist who indeed confirmed that I definitely did *not* have a brain tumor. Not until many, many years later did I realize it was not my fault.

I'm an adult now and have two children. When they were little, they always wondered why I followed them around while they played hide-and-seek. When they were older, I finally told them.

Many often behave according

to others' expectations.

THE EAST HARLEM CENTER

Right before I took a leave of absence from my job in New York City's Garment District and moved to Montana, I volunteered in the evenings for the Children's Aid Society at the East Harlem Center. It was a place for at-risk teenagers to hang out, to keep them off the streets. Having just finished my American Sign Language class at New York University down in Greenwich Village, I applied for a job to work with deaf and hearing-impaired children. Somehow, after speaking with me, however, the head of the Children's Aid Society said they were really in need of help at the East Harlem Center, and I'd be perfect for the task. Whether he pulled a great sales job to convince me or not, and barely knowing what my job would entail, it didn't matter. I immediately accepted the challenge.

The next night, he introduced me to my two bosses. The first was a woman who ran the place. Her name was

Lucia. She was tough and had an edge, maybe because she used to run a prison. The second, her assistant Greg, was a smooth talker. A sensitive kind of guy who was shortly thereafter to become my new boyfriend. Did I mention hot? He was a handsome younger guy seven years my junior.

The first night, Lucia told me that Greg had the night off. She directed me to just walk in and hang out with the kids. That was it—that's all she said, and she left for her office. I would not see her again the entire evening.

I obediently followed her instructions and went to the room where the kids were hanging out. The room was big, open, and cold, both in temperature and décor. The only warmth that filled the room came from the many loud teenagers. The grey walls were completely bare. Some small metal chairs and a couple of metal tables were sporadically placed to complete the façade of a space for human beings. I entered with a smile and tried to talk to a few of them. Some mumbled hi, but most just ignored me. Then a thought came to me. I decided to act upon it. I asked the kids where the bathrooms were, then took off my backpack, which housed my ID, money, credit cards, and all the usual things one carries in a backpack, placed it on the floor, and left the room. I returned about ten minutes later, and to my surprise, they came over to talk to me one by one. The first daring one was Joannie, who I discovered later was the most outspoken of the group. We're still in contact today, thirty-five years later. She came right over to me and told me no one had ever done that before, leaving their bag with them in the room like that. They liked it. "We think you're cool," she said. *They think I'm cool . . . yay!*

I didn't really need the bathroom that night. I only thought that maybe if I could earn their trust—by trusting them—they would talk to me. And that they did.

After working there for a few months, a bond was formed with me and many of the kids. The Children's Aid Society would sometimes give me an allowance to take the teens out. It was never nearly enough, and I always placed a hand into my own pocket. I didn't mind. We had such fun. What a challenging but great group of kids. I often felt their hard exterior was just a protective armor. Even when tempers ran high, I understood.

One night, I had just arrived and heard the thunderous roaring sounds of voices echoing through the halls. Before placing my things down and entering the room, I remembered it was movie night. Those were the days of the VHS (you remember those tapes, right?). As I approached the doorway, I heard Lucia's loud, angry voice yelling at the group, "Who took that movie? I want to know right now!" She harshly told them whoever *stole* the movie wouldn't be allowed back to the center. The vibe in the room was escalating, tensions growing, and voices getting louder. Even Greg's. Everyone seemed to be spiraling out of control.

Suddenly, with a gentle yet commanding voice, I asked Lucia and Greg to please leave the room and give me a moment with the kids—alone. They hesitated for a second, then, with faces still red with anger, fulfilled my request and left. Once alone with the group, I smiled and said hi to everyone. The tensions slowly started to subside. Then, I quietly told the kids that I was going to leave the room and close the door. I wanted whoever took the movie to place it back on top of the television, which was still stationed on the big rolling cart, unmoved. I continued, "And no one is to tell on the person who took it. If anyone tells, they will be the ones to leave the center tonight. Please open the door when you're ready." Then, I left the room and closed the door behind me. A few minutes later, the door opened.

I peeked into the room and saw the movie lying on top of the television. We watched *Beetlejuice* that night. No one had seen it—they loved it!

Later on, Lucia and Greg asked me how I got them to give back the movie. They also asked me who took it.

I told them the very same thing I told the children.

Let us not dim our fire for those

who can't handle our flame.

NO MORE BETRAYALS

When I was young, a certain person in my life constantly undermined my enthusiasm, my zeal for life. At first, I was bewildered—why would someone try to dim my fire? Eventually, it started to wear on me. It didn't feel good. When I was with that person, I began to feel bad about being *me*. Then, it slowly seeped into my daily life, eating away my confidence and self-esteem. I shut down more; it was as if I were a stranger in my own home. It injured my soul. I realized then that I had no room in my life for that negative person who couldn't understand me. Whatever their motives were, it didn't matter anymore.

Empaths—people highly sensitive to what's going on with others—sometimes put up with more than they should. Although we can feel others' pain, it is by no means an excuse to let others try to deflate our balloon, our joy. Rather than discard what served me well and was part of my true nature, I let go of that person.

I finally recognized that for some reason only they knew, or would someday discover, that person was trying to dim my light. All these years later, I still recall the pain of that childhood experience, but I am grateful for what it taught me. When I encounter someone who pushes against my enthusiastic energy, I don't let it sink in. To do otherwise would be to betray my true self. No one lights a lantern to hide it behind a wall.

Not all loners are lonely.

TO THINE OWN SELF BE . . .

Solitude / ˈsä-lə-tūd / *n.* the state of being alone

Loneliness / ˈlōn-lē-nəs / *n.* sadness because
one has no company

I have known both.

It's my solitude, though, that fuels my imagination.
Silence allows me to create. When I'm on a long walk by
myself—a "walking meditation," as I like to call it—creative
ideas just come to me. Or, I should say, through me.

Loner / ˈlōn-ər / *n.* a person who is often alone
or likes to be alone

That's me, even though to the outside world, and maybe
even to those I consider close to me, I do not exemplify "a

loner." One would never know since I can be quite outgoing and friendly. Sometimes, I am even referred to as a social butterfly, and others would definitely describe me as an extrovert. Well, I'm not too sure about that.

When I was younger, I tried not to turn down invitations to parties or get-togethers at bars with friends out of fear I might hurt their feelings if I didn't join. Secretly, I just wanted to stay home and enjoy my solitude, but many times, I forced myself to go, only to come home completely drained and depressed. I never could understand why. I thought something was wrong with me. I felt weird and assumed my friends thought I was, too.

I recall one night when I was older, I had gone to a bar with friends and was having a terrible time. I watched my friends effortlessly talk with guys I had zero interest in interacting with. That didn't stop guys from coming over to talk to me, though. I tried as politely as possible to steer them away. For me, the whole thing felt forced and fake. I didn't like it and went home feeling like the life had been sucked out of me.

EMPATH / 'em-path / *n.* one who absorbs the mental or emotional state of another person or animal or any living thing

Shortly after that evening at the bar, I discovered a new word: empath. So *that's* it, I thought. My lack of ease in social situations came from sensing—feeling—everything going on with the people around me and taking it all in without even knowing it. Realizing this at last made all the difference. It validated who I was. I felt seen and safe, even if it was just a definition printed in a book. I was finally able to embrace who I was, and I slowly started to turn down invitations that I thought would likely be overwhelming for me. The more I accepted who I was and the more authentic I was to myself, the better I felt. That gave me the strength to do what was right for me. I preached to my children the importance of getting to know yourself and then being true to what you know.

That's the key. All my experiences have taught me that when we do that, we can't go wrong.

PART II

SEEING

The world is changing rapidly. People are becoming more aware that intuitive, empathic, and psychic abilities are available to everyone.

It's okay to trust your experiences

as your truth, even when

they defy logic.

THE PLANES

In August 2001, I entertained a houseful of folks at the country house in the Catskill Mountains I shared with my husband, Judd Hirsch. The house was more like a mountaintop retreat with a main house, pool house, playhouse with gym, tennis court, and storybook-type cabins in the woods. Judd was away that summer starring in Yasmina Reza's play *Art* in London. I usually traveled with him when I could but chose to stay back this time with my daughter, Montana, and our new baby boy, London. My guests were relatives of my first husband, Tony: his three sisters, whom I adored; his younger brother; and all their children. Tony and I had been divorced for thirteen years, but the family friendships endured, including the one between me and Tony.

The view from the main house was spectacular. On a clear day, it *did* feel like you could see forever (at least to the Berkshires). I couldn't contain my excitement every morning as I waited for the sun to peak above the horizon and begin the magic show in the sky. The birds singing in the trees must have felt the same way. Up there, the sunrise would flow across the sky in mystic hues of pink and orange while delivering a peaceful greeting to all those watching.

About twenty of us had gathered together at the house in those late, lazy days of August. Tony's family had driven all the way down from Ontario for the camp-like getaway. The adults had just as much fun as the kids, swimming in the pool house, romping in the playhouse, and enjoying outdoor lunches at the long, antique white-marble tables that each easily sat ten. The tables were situated under a beautiful arbor covered in purple wisteria vines. The deck overlooked mounds of soft green mountains. It was a fairytale existence, especially when shared with friends.

One morning, I was on the front deck outside the kitchen, drinking coffee with some of the others, when I noticed a plane in the sky. Although it was too far away for anyone to read the airline's name on it, I pointed at it and alarmingly announced, "Look at that United Airlines plane! There's something wrong with it—it's flying too low!"

But it wasn't low. It was just a faraway passenger jet with the sun hitting its silver hull. The message I felt, however, was that it was flying dangerously low. No one said a word. Then, a series of horrifying thoughts ran through my head.

Oh, no! Something is happening with that plane. There's going to be a war in New York City. I didn't dare repeat those words aloud and risk scaring my seven-year-old daughter, Montana, playing on the deck. We were going back to the city soon to get her ready to start her new school year. Instead, I ran into the house and called Judd in London.

I frantically told him everything about the plane and said I didn't want to go back to the city because something horrible, like a war, was going to happen there. "Let's stay up here and homeschool Montana," I pleaded. He told me to calm down and asked me, "Are you PMS?"

"No!" I replied, still shaken. He said he would be home in just a few days and not to worry; everything would be fine.

Fear continued wracking my body, and I couldn't control my short, gasping breathing. "Everything will be fine," Judd insisted again.

But it wasn't.

After five fun-filled days, the Canadians left, and Judd came home. Once he was settled in and our everyday routines returned, my thoughts of that morning subsided, and I allowed Judd's persuasions to coax me back to the city.

On the morning of September 11, Montana was attending her second half day at Little Dalton in Manhattan, and I was having coffee at Yura Café on Madison Avenue around the corner. Yura was the Little Dalton mothers' hangout. I grabbed a seat outside on one of the metal benches with a few other moms, and we started sharing some of our summer experiences. Suddenly, out of the blue, I felt compelled to open up and tell them my vision of the plane and my fear of a war in the city. As our discussion about what I had just revealed started to take off, our phones began ringing incessantly. We were told that a plane had just crashed into one of the towers at the World Trade Center. Our callers relayed the news that it was an American Airlines plane and the crash was thought to be an accident. My hands started to shake, and the inside of my body ached as if a massive bruise was working its way through every tissue.

Looking down Madison Avenue from 91st Street, we could already see the smoke rising in the air from nearly six miles away. We huddled together, in shock and almost unable to move. About twenty minutes later, we received more calls and learned that the other tower had now been hit—this time by a *United Airlines* plane. The reports declared it was no accident, and everyone started to panic. By the time we received a call from Dalton's emergency hotline, we were already at the school door waiting to pick up our little ones.

After Montana was safely with me, I called Judd, who was headed upstate. He quickly turned around to get us, and we escaped the city just before they closed the bridges and tunnels. About three hours later, we were back in our Catskills home, feeling blessed to have such a sanctuary to escape to. Judd and I got things ready to put up some friends who also wanted to flee the city.

It was an anxious, mind-numbing time for all. I later learned that my first high school crush died in the towers that day, along with the many others who also perished. I felt helpless and confused. Why was I only able to "see" bits and pieces—why couldn't I have foreseen the whole thing?

Maybe I could have stopped it, warned someone, somewhere, somehow. These questions haunt me to this day.

When my children were younger, they split their time between me and Judd during their winter holidays, as set in our divorce agreement. I always brought the children upstate to celebrate Hanukkah and Christmas, where we would be cozy in our log cabin in the woods with a magnificent view of the mountains covered in snow. The house beamed with warmth from the golden glow of the wood stove and multi-colored lights and the soft scent of the seven-foot balsam fir. Judd would pick up the kids for the rest of the holiday, and off they'd go to a warm place in the Caribbean to celebrate the new year. When I was married to Judd, we usually visited a Caribbean island twice a year, so he continued the tradition and usually brought them to a different island each holiday. One year, they went to St. Croix for the first time.

On January 2, I was already back in the city in my Upper East Side apartment. While reading on the couch early that morning, a thought suddenly flashed through my head—something was wrong with my children. I felt it, and I panicked. I called Judd and the children, but no one answered. It was only an hour later in St. Croix, so it was early there, too. Maybe their phones were still off for the night. I couldn't shake this bad feeling, so I called my mother in Los Angeles, where it was 5:00 a.m. I woke her and rambled on and on about something being wrong and not being able to reach them. My mom tried her best to calm me down, saying, "Oh, they're probably out for breakfast or something."

"No!" I screamed. Then another thought struck me, and I said, "Sorry, but I have to hang up and put them in a bubble!" She probably had no idea what I was talking about because neither did I. I ended the call and followed the inkling to close my eyes and picture my children in a protective bubble where no harm could come to them. I held this image for a while, and when I finished, I felt a little better. An hour or so later, I finally got through, and everything was fine. I have no idea how or from where that idea about the bubble came to me.

Two days after they returned from St. Croix, I was having dinner at the table with my children, and London said, "Mom, you're not going to believe what happened to us in St. Croix! We were driving one morning, and a big white truck coming in the other direction skidded into our lane as the driver headed around the curve. We all screamed because we thought he was going to crash right into us! At the very last second, the driver swerved back into his own lane."

"What?" I asked, alarmed. "That's so scary!"

"Yeah," he said. "We thought we were going to die."

Then it hit me.

I asked them both, "Do you remember what day that was? What was the date?"

Montana thought for a moment and then said, "January 2nd."

I couldn't believe it! I told them the whole story of how that same morning I felt something was wrong. I tried to call, but when I couldn't reach them, I felt compelled to imagine them in a transparent bubble that would protect them. They were amazed. After their initial shock and questions, we ate in silence, all of us soaking in the mysterious event.

The dinner table had never been so quiet.

We are all boundless beings

with infinite potential.

FIRST VISION,
BROOKLYN STYLE

In my early thirties, I started dating a guy I had met on Dog Hill in New York City. Dog lovers met on this big, grassy, inviting hill located just inside Central Park on East 79th Street near Fifth Avenue to socialize and let our dogs run and frolic off-leash. It was a fun spot, and not just for the dogs.

One afternoon in late spring, the group I came with dispersed, each obediently following our dogs like we were playing follow the leader. While running after my pup, I stumbled across a guy who stopped me in my tracks. Although he was cute, what really caught my eye was the huge snake wound around his shoulders. I was petrified of snakes and couldn't take my eyes off the two of them. He saw me staring and gave me a sweet, flirty smile. After he returned the snake to his friend, the rightful owner, he approached me. In a charming French accent, he introduced himself as Jean Paul from Paris, and I immediately became completely enamored. We started dating.

It was spring, but the flowers weren't the only items blooming. By early summer, Jean Paul and I were an item. We were always together. He sold antiques worldwide, so he could work from wherever he wanted. Few, including myself, could do that in those days. I worked in the Garment District, showing up in an office in the heart of New York's famous fashion industry every day.

One cloudless Friday, I played hooky, and we headed out to eastern Long Island to stay on Jean Paul's sailboat docked in Sag Harbor. I packed up my things along with my two dogs, and we set off in my bright red truck. Jean Paul owned the boat with his good friend Christoff, who was also a Parisian. It was a pretty, thirty-five-foot sailboat with dark wooden floors in the interior. They were in the process of fixing it up so they could sail around the world. *How exciting,* I thought.

After a fun-filled day of Jet Skiing and working on the boat, mainly on the nonexistent kitchen that needed to be fabricated and assembled, the three of us had dinner at a lovely local pizza joint in town.

Afterward, exhausted from the day's activities, Jean Paul and I chose to retire and go straight to bed. The only bedroom was under the boat's bridge, which became our comfy little cave. While I was drifting off to sleep that night, I had my first of what would be many visions throughout my life. Startled, I woke up Jean Paul. "I saw a man with a shotgun," I said excitedly. "He was in a building holding people hostage. Three shots rang out, but nobody was hurt." Seeing my discomfort and anxiety, he threw his protective arms around me and said it was probably just a bad dream. I told him I didn't think I was sleeping. He held me tighter, and I fell asleep in the safety of his warm embrace.

The next morning, Jean Paul went to the nearby 7-Eleven to pick up coffee and bagels. He came back with a strange look on his face. "Look at this," he said as he handed me the morning newspaper. Blaring from the front page of the *New York Post* was the headline, "GUNMAN IN BROOKLYN HOLDS PEOPLE HOSTAGE." He had fired three shots before he gave himself up, the article reported, and no one was hurt.

"What?" I shrieked. "That's crazy—that's what my vision was last night!" We both stared at the paper, stunned.

Months later, once their work was completed and the boat was ready to sail, Jean Paul and Christoff invited me to join them on their year's journey around the world. Although tempted, I declined. Maybe it should have been a harder decision, but it wasn't. I had two dogs that were like my children; they were not invited. End of story. And so, that was the end of our lucid love affair.

Every experience has the power

to transform you.

THE NUMBER-FIVE HORSE

One summer in my single days, my friend Peter, who lived next door to me in a prewar apartment building on a charming, quiet, tree-lined street located on the Upper East Side of Manhattan, invited me to join him and a large group of his friends for the weekend at the house they had rented for the summer on Long Island. The house was in West Hampton, a small hamlet known for its pretty beaches, laid-back atmosphere, and fun bars and restaurants. It's always been a favorite summer destination for New Yorkers to relax, socialize, and escape the city heat. Peter and I had become very close friends, even though we couldn't be more different. He was a handsome, business-suit, financial kind of guy, and I was, well, a whimsical, spontaneous, free spirit working in the fashion industry. I think Peter and I bonded over our failed loved affairs and other heartbreaks we shared with one another.

I packed up my two-door Chevy Blazer, which, at that time, everyone called a "truck" because SUVs weren't trendy yet. My dogs happily jumped in the back seat alongside my weekend-getaway backpack stuffed with sunblock, a baseball cap, a bikini, gauzy and semi-sheer summer tops, jeans, and a casual skirt. I stopped at a Dunkin' Donuts (this was pre-Starbucks), grabbed a coffee and a bran muffin, and headed out.

I arrived early that Saturday morning, and after brief introductions, we decided as a group to spend the day at the beach. I anticipated the peaceful delight of breathing in the scent of the salty sea, which reminded me of family outings long ago. Some of us took walks along the shore, while others went swimming in the restless waves, read a book, or joined a pickup volleyball game. I participated in everything except swimming—I had feared getting into the water ever since surviving a near-fatal swimming accident when I was younger. We were a large group of at least twenty, and I still have the picture of us together on the beach taken that first day.

Sometime that morning, I overheard talk about the Belmont Stakes, the horse race that would take place later that day. The race is part of the Triple Crown, made up of the Preakness, the shortest race of the group; the Kentucky Derby, the most famous; and the Belmont, the longest of the three. These races were usually limited to three-year-old

Thoroughbreds, and while I wasn't paying much attention to them that year, I had enjoyed the few times I'd watched the Kentucky Derby on TV. As the sun began to dip into the horizon, we packed up our beach paraphernalia and headed for our cars. While standing in the middle of the hot parking lot, I had a vision. The scene played out in my mind like a movie: the number-five horse in a race crossed the finish line, winning the race. I immediately recalled the earlier conversations on the beach about the Belmont Stakes. Did I just see the winner of the upcoming race?

I dared not say anything because I didn't want anyone to think I was crazy. Instead, I loudly blurted out across the parking lot, "Does anyone know the name of the number-five horse racing today?" A few mumbled no, and the rest didn't answer. No one knew. Peter and I said our goodbyes to the group and told them we'd catch up with them later that evening.

My friend Julie was having her wedding shower about sixty miles away that night, and I had convinced Peter to join me. Afterward, Peter and I drove the hour back to Westhampton Beach. As a thank-you for joining me at Julie's event, I bought him a drink at the bar near his rented place. When we returned to the huge house, I learned I was supposed to share a bedroom with Peter's friend Tom, but I chose to sleep on the porch in the snug hammock instead. I have always loved sleeping under the stars. That night, the many stars shone brightly, and I quickly fell asleep under their protective blanket.

The next morning, I awoke to some early risers spilling onto the veranda, sipping their coffee and enjoying their conversations with their meal. I was hungry because I hadn't eaten much the night before, so I left to get some breakfast at the cute restaurant a few steps from the house. I returned with a black coffee and two fried eggs on a kaiser roll and sat on the steps next to a girl named Betsy, who had joined the morning gathering. She was outgoing and one of the friendliest toward me. As the only one in the group who didn't know anyone, I appreciated her amicable gestures. Until that moment, I had forgotten about the horse race, and suddenly struck with curiosity about my vision, I asked, "Does anyone know who won the Belmont Stakes yesterday?" Betsy looked at me wide-eyed and said emphatically for all to hear, "You said it yesterday, Bonni, the number-five horse! Hansel! How did you know that?"

My head was spinning. That was only the second vision I'd ever had, so I was still new to the experience. But I felt especially comfortable in my own skin that morning—even among a group of strangers—so I told them exactly what took place in the parking lot the day before. The looks on their faces were priceless. Many didn't say much, but Betsy seemed fascinated. She leaned closer and quietly asked me a lot of questions about it.

There's always at least one in a crowd who is open to the mysteries of life, a curious soul eager to hear more about the strange yet undeniably real things human beings can experience.

A few months later, I was fast asleep in my Upper East Side apartment next door to Peter's. Suddenly, I realized I was hovering by the top of my bedroom window shade, looking out at the night sky illuminated by the city lights in the distance. My building was on a side street, and my apartment faced the back, so I felt lucky to have a quiet place with only gardens below me. I turned away from the window to look at my bed and saw myself sleeping there. After turning again to gaze out the top of the window, panic set in. I recognized that I was not in my body. As my fear heightened, I told myself over and over to lift my arm. Then, in an instant, I was back in my body, and sure enough, I lifted my arm. That was my first out-of-body experience. Looking back, I wish I hadn't freaked out and instead been able to enjoy the moment and see where the adventure would have taken me.

When we collect moments,

we fill up our lives with joy.

JUST LIKE WALTON

Years ago, I went to the movies with one of my friends. There, I took notice of a younger, quite handsome guy taking our tickets. His chiseled features and strong body were complemented by his thick, wavy blond hair that flowed past his broad shoulders. It was more than his sexy good looks that caught my attention; I could tell he was deaf because of the way he spoke and how his eyes followed my lips when I asked him a question. I had just completed an American Sign Language class at New York University. In sign, I asked him, "Are you deaf?" He answered back with a shake of his closed fist, "Yes." I signed "hello" and my name letter by letter, and we had a quick encounter using our non-verbal language skills led by our hands, faces, and bodies. It was a direct passage from one to the other.

After the movie was over, on our way out of the theatre, my eyes searched for him, darting all over like a mantis shrimp frantically seeking a meal. My eyes finally landed on his as his were searching for mine. He sauntered over and flashed a smile that could brighten a stormy day.

We signed a bit more, although I don't remember what about. He asked for my phone number and explained to me that we would be able to communicate by telephone. He gave me a special number to use, as he had a TTY (teletype) machine that enabled him to read my words and have a translator speak his words to me. I had never talked with a deaf person on the phone before. Discovering how tech would allow us two strangers with different ways of communicating to connect was an eye-opening experience. We talked on the phone the next night. Our conversation lasted over an hour. He asked me out. I gladly went. He was so cute and so nice—how could I not!

Our first date was a picnic at Battery Park downtown. After we finished our sandwiches, we just lay in the grass, gazing upward, signing to one another, our arms stretched high as if we were signing to the sky. That day, the sun warmed our bodies along with our hearts.

As the days and nights went by, Walton and I continued to spend more and more time with each other. We had fun taking little trips together. Once, on the shores of Long Is-land, Walton ventured into the salty waters as I stood by the shore, dipping my feet in and watching the big, boisterous waves roll back and forth. They were both mesmerizing, the man and the sea.

I stood at the tip of the water wondering what living a life in silence would be like. Then, for a moment, but what seemed like an eternity, the sounds of the crashing waves were no longer in my ear. Awestruck, I heard nothing while the big threatening waves carried on. The experience was so quick I did not have time to be nervous (and I can be a nervous person). The only feeling I was left with was gratitude for experiencing, at least for a second, what it might be like to be Walton. I understood it was only a quick snapshot and not the reality of being Walton, who navigates those waters every day.

When Walton got out of the ocean, I shared my crazy experience with him. He was amazed, and I was astounded he actually asked me out again.

Nothing material in this world

can compare to a beautiful experience.

STARRY NIGHT

It was an exciting time for me. I had recently ended a seven-year on-and-off relationship with a man I had finally laid to rest not only in my mind but in my heart. My mom constantly told me that Prince Charming wouldn't come knocking at my door, so I needed to get out there. I was surprised she knew so much about dating trends in the digital age. "Go on one of those dating sites," she'd say. I argued that all I wanted to do now was concentrate on my kids, and if I met someone great, it would happen organically. I was wasting my breath. If your mother is like mine, you know how relentless they can be. She didn't stop. Every time we spoke, she brought up the same subject.

One evening I lightheartedly brought up the situation with my daughter and told her I'd just tell her grandmother, her Nanny, that I had signed up on one of the dating sites. Maybe then she'd let it go. My daughter looked at me, shocked, and said, "But, Mom, you don't lie!" Oy. She was right.

I gave in, worked up an online dating profile, and registered on one of the dating sites so I wouldn't have to lie to my mom or disillusion my daughter.

The second person I agreed to meet on the site introduced himself as Bobby. I told my mom, friends, and kids how nice he was but that I just liked him as a friend. Bobby continued to pursue me, and although I was convinced this would remain a friendship *only*—you guessed it. Love found a way.

On our fourth official date, we had dinner at one of my favorite neighborhood Italian restaurants I often visited with my kids. They made the best Caesar salad, and I loved the orecchiette pasta, the southern Italian specialty with broccoli rabe and shaved parmesan cheese, which I ordered that night. My date, being more traditional than I, ordered the lasagna. He offered me a taste, but I was already off meat by then, so I declined. He had no desire to taste my dish either. Maybe the limp, seaweed-green broccoli put him off. We talked about our past marriages, our kids, and the things that spoke to our hearts. I didn't, however, share with him my many strange and wondrous visions or out-of-body experiences. I didn't want to scare him away too quickly. That was about to change.

After a few hours of eating, sharing, laughing, and sipping our wine, it was time to go home. Bobby offered to join me in taking my dog, Shanti, for a walk. So we walked and talked and lost track of time. He usually drove back to Connecticut, but being that it was so late and we were exhausted, I told him he could stay the night.

We were lying in bed, talking and waiting for sleep to descend upon us. The next thing I remember was Bobby gently shaking me, saying, "Bonni, Bonni, are you okay?"

"Yeah," I muttered. "What happened?" He told me he was talking to me, and when I didn't answer, he looked over to see if I was asleep. My eyes were wide open, staring blankly at the ceiling, and I had a blissful smile on my face. He kept saying my name, but when I still wouldn't answer, he got nervous and shook me. "I was a star," I kept repeating, still a bit dazed. "It was so beautiful. I was a star, and darkness was all around me. There was no earth, but other bright stars were there, too, and I recognized some of them. We knew each other. Occasionally, one even flew right by me."

I turned my head to look at him. "It was so beautiful," I whispered again.

Still a bit dreamy-foggy and not thinking about how my new suitor would take all this, I continued to spill it out exactly as it was. How I was a star in the velvet darkness and everything was alive and connected. How astronomer Carl Sagan said we are all stardust . . . the elements that make us were created in stars over four billion years ago, and somewhere deep inside, we know this and long to return to them. When I finished, I expected him to give me some excuse and fly out the door. He stayed.

Nine months later, Bobby became husband number three. And we're still married today.

The power of our thoughts

can change our reality.

CHICKS AND TIX

Psychokinesis / sī-kō-kə-'nē-səs / *n.* the ability
of the mind to change the state or position of a
physical object

In 1986, French scientist Rene Peoc'h, Ph.D., conducted a fascinating experiment to expand on the parapsychology research that began in the 1970s. Parapsychology, the study of psychokinesis and other "paranormal" activities like telepathy and precognition, had finally brought science into the mix of these "gifts." Peoc'h wanted to find out if chicks could affect the movement of a small robot built to glide around on a table in front of their cage. Chicks, like most birds, imprint on the first thing they see after they hatch, attaching to it as their mother. In his experiment, Peoc'h found that the chicks not only imprinted on the little robot (that looked like the metal version of a small take-out container for soup) but also caused the robot to spend most of its time near their cage. As the chicks longed to be closer to their mother, their thoughts attracted the robot to them. Although the robot was programmed to move randomly, the chicks' mind power overcame that.

To check the results in another way, Peoc'h ran another experiment with chicks that had *not* imprinted on the robot, and the robot's movement stayed random. Peoc'h ran many more studies over the years that confirmed these findings time after time.

These kinds of experiments show that paranormal "psychic powers" are normal after all. Knowing this helps me feel less crazy when I do certain things . . . like the time I got a pickup moving again without any tools except my intention.

I was upstate at my house when my husband, Bobby, and I decided to give my daughter, Montana, a driving lesson. It's a great place to learn and practice driving. The country roads are so beautiful and have hardly any traffic. Perfect for a driving lesson, that is, unless I'm sitting in front. I get too nervous and could make any driver crazy. (I have since gotten better, though, and my daughter, who is now thirty, even complimented me on how calm I was when she recently drove through a torrential rainstorm when I visited her in Minneapolis.) That day, I was barred from the front and got ready to cram into the back seat of Bobby's old, beat-up, blue pickup truck with my young son, London. The back seat was so small I felt like a contortionist as I twisted my body to slip into it. My husband sat in the front passenger seat.

Upon descending the long, winding driveway, the steering wheel suddenly got stuck. Montana immediately braked and stopped the car. Smart girl. As always. My husband, being very handy in all areas, tried to fix the problem but couldn't. He couldn't even figure out what was wrong. The steering wheel just wouldn't budge. After about twenty minutes of his kind but fruitless efforts, I asked everyone to please step out of the truck for a second and move back a bit.

Once they were gone, I glided into the driver's seat, closed the door, and placed both hands on the steering wheel. I caressed it lovingly, slowly moving my hands up and down around it. Right away, I felt heat rising in my hands. Then I said, out loud, "You will move now. Thank you so much for moving." I repeated these gestures and sentences many times, and sure enough, after a few minutes, the steering wheel moved!

Knowing all the stunts I had performed over the years, my family was not surprised at all. They giggled as we piled back into the truck to continue Montana's driving lesson.

Even after fixing a steering wheel with my mind, I still doubted myself. Who knows, maybe that keeps me in check.

But soon after that interesting driving lesson, I set out yet again to prove the power of thought. The train experiment always did the trick.

I boarded the train to Manhattan at an off-peak hour when it wasn't crowded and took a seat in my favorite area, where three seats face each other. A young man was sitting in the window seat, so I took the aisle to leave a space between us. The guy was leaning his head against the window. Although he looked to be in his twenties, he seemed more like a child of the sixties. He had thick, wavy, blond hair to his shoulders and wore a yellow tie-dyed T-shirt with a black peace sign on the front and ripped blue jeans. His ticket was already punched out and in clear view, protruding from the ticket slot on top of his seat. I almost asked him where he bought his cool jeans, but I didn't want to get distracted from my mission.

I wanted to prove to myself how powerful our thoughts are. How they are energy, and how that energy affects things around us. As the train started moving and the woman came up the aisle to collect the tickets, I said the same thing to myself that I always do in this experiment: *I'm invisible to her. The railway ticket conductor will not ask me for my ticket. She will walk past me as if I'm not there. She will not ask me for my ticket.* I repeated this mantra over and over. And she did indeed walk right past me without asking me for my ticket. She even passed me three more times before we reached

Manhattan. A sixty minute trip, and I was never asked for my ticket. Even my son bore witness to this a few times. I would say, "Watch this—they'll walk right past me and not ask me for my ticket." And to his surprise, they always did.

I got my proof that day as I had on other days, but it's funny—no matter how many times I do this experiment and it works, I'm still flabbergasted.

When my daughter, Montana, was sixteen, we lived a short walk from her high school, and she and a few of her girl-friends loved to come over on their lunch break to eat the homemade vegetarian lasagna awaiting them. Sometimes, they came after school to have a snack and do their home-work at the table in our comfy, hang-out-style dining room.

One March day in 2011, the girls came for lunch and, after throwing their heavy backpacks filled with books onto Montana's bed, joined me in the kitchen to help set the table. While pulling out the silverware, one of Montana's closest friends asked me why I'd texted Monti (her nickname) many times that day to see if she was okay. Forgetting this was more than Montana's usual crew because there was a new girl in the mix who didn't know me very well, I casually turned to my daughter and said, "Oh, sorry. I was projecting my worried feeling onto you. Something bad is going to happen in the world, like a big natural disaster." The new girl looked frightened, but I couldn't tell if she was afraid of what I'd just said or of me. I think it was probably the latter. I told them not to worry—it wasn't going to happen in this country. Seeing her friend turn pale at my outburst, Montana told her, "Don't worry, that's just what my mom does. She knows things sometimes."

The next day, on Friday, March 11, a tsunami hit Japan.

What Montana didn't tell her new friend because I tried to keep it under wraps was that when I get these feelings, I feel them in my gut and get shaky and upset. My mom was the only person I always called when I had one of these visions, even about 9/11. I had also called her about the natural disaster that March. "Is it going to be in LA?" she asked emphatically. (That's where she lived.) I couldn't help but laugh and told her not to worry because, just as I had told Montana and her friends, it would not happen in this country.

The doors to higher vibrations are open;

all we have to do is enter.

THE RIGHT BLEND

I used to speak to my mom at least two times a day. Every day. We lived three thousand miles away from each other, but one would never know. Our close bond started when I was just a little girl, and it only grew from there. I felt so lucky to have had my mom on this earth for so long. She lived for eighty-eight years and died during the height of COVID-19.

Although one might think the opposite, I believe the older you get, the more you love, appreciate, and at times even *need* your mom. I still need mine. We were always there for each other. She was my best friend. How I miss her voice—she had one of those distinct, low, youthful voices that always seemed to raise the spirits of others by the sheer tone of it.

I kept many of her spry, raspy phone messages. They're still on my iPhone, and I won't delete them. Erasing them would be like placing a block of ice in the sun that you want to keep frozen. Her voice is now in my imaginary freezer. My memories of her, my love for her . . . the void inside slowly subsides but never fully goes away. I shouldn't complain, though, because she does leave signs. Surprising and mysterious signs.

One day, while I was making my usual breakfast, a fruit smoothie filled with a handful of arugula, I began thinking about my mom. I did that quite often those days, as she had recently passed away. She died during the pandemic lockdown, so I didn't even get to say goodbye in person. I lived in the East and she in the West, and the planes weren't flying.

I remember missing her so much that day. As I stood by the quartz counter preparing my breakfast, I thought about how I wished I could talk to her, and my eyes started tearing. As I investigated the contents in my blender, I saw what looked like a yellow label, so I reached in, wondering how it got there. I pulled out something that wasn't a label at all but a piece of yellow-tinted arugula in the shape of a beautiful heart! My mom used to send me yellow roses every year for my birthday. I knew immediately that it was a sign from her. A sign that she heard me. That she always hears me. I took a photo of that delicate leaf to keep as a reminder.

I then placed the lovely, tender leaf on top of an orange lid I had put on the counter. Forgetting it was there, I carelessly screwed the orange lid over the Ball jar filled with sweet potato puree, which I sometimes added to my smoothies. (I know it's over the top, but I like to match the lid with the contents of the jar when possible. It's easier to recognize what I'm looking for in the refrigerator). I placed the jar in the fridge and forgot about it.

A few hours later, when I realized what I had done, I ran back to the kitchen, fearing the sign from my mother was gone, wiped away by my hand on the jar and lost. I flung the refrigerator doors open, and to my astonishment, it was still there, resting just where I had set it on top of the orange lid.

Signs come to me in many different shapes, sizes, and places. When I'm open to receive, they appear. As I write this, I wonder how my mom will show up next.

One warm July day in Connecticut, a month after my mom passed away, seemed the perfect time to dine outside with my husband and son in the late afternoon as the sun began to dip behind the trees. We had just inherited a bigger barbeque from a neighbor and were anxious to try it out. We made the meal and set everything on the black wrought iron table shaded from the sultry sun by a sage-green umbrella. While munching on my veggie burger, my thoughts again turned to my mom. Just as I was telling my husband and son how much I wished I could get a sign from her, I happened to glance up at our bird feeder hanging on a metal pole about ten feet away. I noticed a small, all-white bird I had never seen before.

"Look! Look at that bird!" I announced excitedly as I pointed in its direction. We were all taken with the winged little creature. My husband, who had lived in that house for over thirty-five years, said he had never seen a bird like that before. So, when we finished our burgers, hot dogs, beans, and corn, I looked up the bird and learned it was an albino house sparrow. The description stated they are one in a million, so sightings are extremely rare. When the bird flew away, I looked up at the sky and quietly thanked the universe and my mom for giving me the sign I needed that day.

Six months after my mom died, the pain of that open wound had not started to heal. Not one bit. This was around the holidays when I would always give our mailperson at the time (they changed often in our neighborhood) a holiday card filled with good cheer and a monetary gift. That year, I was late with my card and apologized to the tall, handsome mail carrier whose name I didn't know. His thick blond hair complemented his muscular build and angular face. Whenever I saw him during my daily neighborhood walk, he waved from across the street or, if we met on the sidewalk, said hello with his lovely Dutch accent. One day, when our paths crossed, I mentioned that I had left something for him in the mailbox. I knew he got it, for when I returned, it was gone.

The next day, I went for a walk to the nearby beach. The path by the sound was wild and rugged beneath my feet, and a gentle breeze washed across my face. The fresh, clean air smelled like the sea as I stepped toward the jagged boulders, my favorite part of the walk, but even that couldn't cheer up the sadness in my heart. I missed my mother so much. I couldn't help the salty tears that mirrored the ocean at high tide. They overflowed and cascaded down my already wet cheeks. I had thought about my mom that entire day—she couldn't escape my thoughts. Not that I wanted her to. I wanted a sign from her. Just one sign. I went home with a heavy heart.

Once back in the house, I realized I had forgotten to collect the mail, which is always placed in a small periwinkle basket nailed by the door. I went back and grabbed the only envelope in the box. Written on the solid white envelope, the kind that encloses a card, was my first name. I opened it while walking back into the house and read the brief note: "Bonni, thank you so much for the holiday gift. Audrey."

This thank-you from my mail carrier revealed his name to me for the first time. What?! Audrey was my mom's name! Tears flowed down my cheeks. I knew it was a sign from her—only my mom could have finagled that kind of special delivery.

~ঌ

A few years ago, a friend of mine I had known for about eight years had just passed. She was constantly on my mind and in my heart, and I often wished I could get a sign from her as well. I had been to her apartment only once because her partner worked there, and she preferred to meet at my apartment or go out for a meal. Because of COVID-19 restrictions and her vulnerability due to her illness, for the last two years of her life, our friendship was limited to speaking over the phone, which we did at least twice a week. Our talks were anything but limited, though. We shared our thoughts on practically everything under the sun, including the afterlife. Our conversations were deep, lengthy, and filled with ideas.

One day, about a month after she was gone, I was taking one of my nieces out for breakfast. Saying we both loved bagels, especially New York bagels, is an understatement, but she can't eat dairy, and I can't eat gluten. That's why she couldn't wait to introduce me to her dream bagel place where we could get vegan, gluten-free bagels that were so delicious that even her full-gluten-and-dairy-eating partner loved them. I was skeptical, but at the same time, I couldn't wait to find out if they were as good as she said. I had tried a *lot* of gluten-free bagels, and none of them appealed to my taste buds. Happily—magically—the bagels were as divine as she promised. I ordered two, smeared with cream cheese and lox. Okay, enough about the bagels already.

We decided to eat at my niece's apartment, which was only a short distance away. While we were walking and talking, for some reason I took my gaze off her face and looked up. Right in front of me stood my departed friend's apartment building, 777!

I knew it was a sign from her. What more can you ask of such a magical morning?

A week later, I was meeting a family friend I hadn't seen in many years. Our fathers had met at camp when they were kids, so we had known each other for a long time. She came into the city from Upstate New York to have lunch, and we decided to stay in my apartment and enjoy Japanese food delivered from a neighborhood restaurant. While chatting over luscious edamame, sushi, and miso soup, she started talking about the years she lived in the city and how she was on the board of her building, which she named.

No way.

That was the same building as my friend who had recently passed—777! And my friend eating lunch with me that day not only lived in the same building as my other friend, but they also shared the same first name.

One day, while driving my red Subaru (I like red cars) and playing music from my Spotify playlist (which consists of over 650 songs), my thoughts again turned to my mom. I became heartbroken recalling something I had wanted to share with her but never had the chance to do so. I felt a sadness come over me like I do on many occasions when I think about my mom. The void feels like an empty hole. As I started to tear up, Debussy's "Clair de lune" came on.

I grew up taking piano lessons from a woman who banged my hand on the piano when I made a mistake. I didn't like those lessons at all. My father, on the other hand, who had never taken a music lesson in his life, used to play by ear and even wrote a few songs himself. One of them, called "Little Children," was my favorite. It was about us kids . . . as well as his lost youth. I can play it by heart, and whenever I see a piano, I take the opportunity to do so. Maybe I'm afraid I'll forget the song if I don't, which would be like losing a piece of my dad.

Not knowing the names of notes or anything else about music, my dad would sit down at the piano and create a beautiful piece of music. Then, he would write down the words as he slowly played. I loved sitting on the couch in our green-carpeted living room, perpendicular to the piano so that I could watch him at his mastery. Sometimes I stood right next to him, mesmerized as I watched his fingers slide effortlessly across the keys, as if his talent was contagious and maybe I'd catch it.

My mom, however, had taken piano lessons for years as a young girl but could only remember one piece she'd learned. When I was a child, I heard her play that one song every day, "Clair de lune" by Debussy! I know my mom heard my thoughts about her that afternoon as I drove down that lonesome highway. It comforted me and brought me joy to know that they *can* hear us.

A minute or two after I finished writing this, a woman who had worked for my dad for twenty years, some of which overlapped with the time I worked for him, too (we both adored her), phoned out of the blue. She told me she had run into a mutual friend I'd introduced her to years ago. They both still work in the Garment District. That made her think of me, so she decided to call. We hadn't spoken since my dad died thirteen years ago. I had just finished silently thanking my dad for the many things he taught me, especially his love for literature, art, music, and all those great old movies. Bette Davis was our specialty, as we often watched her movies together. *Now, Voyager* was our favorite. Then she called. I took that heartwarming, synchronistic moment as a direct sign from my dad.

They really *do* hear us.

PART III

GIFTS IN KIND

One single act of kindness

grows new seeds.

Searching for happiness is like trying to capture air in a net. Happiness is the experience we get as a gift when we live a life filled with love, kindness, and gratitude.

NO SMALL CHANGE

When I was twenty-nine years old, I went through what I consider an early mid-life crisis. I was working at the time in a high-powered, high-paying showroom in New York City's Garment District. But feeling something was missing in my life, I signed up for a Voyageur Outward Bound course in northern Minnesota. For a few weeks, I lived in the woods, canoed the Boundary Waters, hiked and rock climbed, and was left on an island for three days and three nights, truly enjoying and living life to the fullest with what some would consider nothing. While away, I developed a painful infection on my foot but dared not say anything because I didn't want to be sent home. I felt so free, so *me*. I had discovered a strength within that I didn't know existed.

Once back in New York City, I saw a doctor who treated my foot. While hobbling home with my new bandage, I passed three homeless men on the street who caught my

attention. I was drawn to them, wanting to better understand and learn about their circumstances. I always traveled
with a notebook and camera, and I politely asked if I could
spend the day writing about them. One man asked if I was
a reporter, and I explained I was just a regular girl.

These three men took me into the fold and couldn't
wait to tell me their stories. I was left recalling the sense
of camaraderie they not only shared between themselves
but extended to me as well. And I will never forget two
experiences from that indelible day.

I had wanted to document my new acquaintances and
asked passersby if they would please take our picture together. Everyone ignored or avoided us fearfully. Some
even made a half circle to prevent coming too close. Finally,
one of the homeless men in our group offered to take the
picture. I remain struck by the sense of isolation that these
men endured on a daily basis.

Donnie shared with me how he ended up on the street.
He lost his full-time job, and then his home, and then his
wife left him with their only child. With no money, no
family, and nowhere to go, he became homeless. I will also
never forget the ultimate act of sharing I experienced that
afternoon. Donnie, who seemed to be the group's leader,
was responsible for collecting the change thrown our way.
When a stranger tossed us a handful of coins, Donnie handed
one to each of us—including me. I was so taken by that

moment. Someone who had so little had the generosity of heart and spirit to share their humble bounty, even though he knew I was not homeless.

Each day I try to keep this memory close to my heart. I wonder about the many ways we might give to other human beings—not just through money but compassion, time, and a shoulder to cry on. Donnie cried his story on mine as we sat against the wall that day. Not only did these men welcome me, a complete stranger, into their group, but they embraced me as if I were one of them. That's an honor I have never forgotten.

~~~

The other night, as I was walking my dog, Shanti, on the Upper East Side of Manhattan, I heard a man talking in a loud, pleading voice, "Doesn't anybody hear me?" The block was desolate, dimly lit, so I couldn't see him at first. Oh, but I *heard* him. Every cell in my body heard him. "Doesn't anybody see me? All I want is a bag of Cheetos. I only want a bag of Cheetos."

I had already walked past him but knew that on my way back I would stop by the shadow of a man I saw sitting on a wooden flower box. It was then I heard it. I don't think I'll ever forget his words. His words went right to my heart. "Doesn't anybody even know I *exist?*" Upon hearing that,
~~~

I turned around and walked over to the man on the box, looked down into his sad eyes, and reached my hand out for his. Our hands became entwined as if we were old friends. I spoke gently. "I know you exist." Tears streamed down his cheek as he gazed into my eyes. "Thank you," he said. We stayed like that for a bit, and when he slowly released my hand, I reached into my pocket and handed him the only bill inside. "Thank you," he said again.

Kindness invites miracles.

ON THE SAME PAGE

Living in New York City, I meet all kinds of people of all ages and from all walks of life. Years before I got into energy healing, I was walking across town on a side street somewhere in the East 80s between Lexington and Third Avenues. A small, quaint coffee house was tucked away beneath the massive building on top of it. I loved their coffee as well as this hidden gem's cozy atmosphere.

Upon descending the five steps and entering the café, I was immediately transported into another world. The warm red velvet curtains that cascaded onto the floor and the plush, orange and green wingback chairs gave me the feeling of being in an old European town. Yet I felt right at home.

After my body slid into one of the comfy chairs, I smiled sweetly at the other patrons as I eyed the chocolate cookies lining the glass counter. I sunk deeper and deeper into the chair like I would the warm, trusting arms of a lover.

I took out a book to read. I always carry a book in my backpack. It's a friend I like to keep close to—I take every opportunity to read, no matter where I am. Yes, I do have a Kindle, but I love cradling a book in the palms of my hands, caressing its pages with my fingers, and smelling the scent of the paper. When I finally finished drinking my coffee in my little private womb of that enchanting coffee house, I decided to head home to regroup before picking up my daughter from school.

On the way home, I noticed a young girl sitting on a bench. She looked about sixteen or seventeen years old. I read her features and could sense she was unhappy. I went over to sit beside her and told her I liked her ring. It was a cool silver ring shaped like a snake with ruby-red eyes. I introduced myself—"Hi, I'm Bonni."

"I'm Blaire."

I thought I'd break the ice, so I started to tell her a bit about my life. How I came from divorced parents and was in my second marriage, married to the father of my two young children. How I loved animals and we had two dogs, two tortoises, two beta fish, a degu . . .

While I continued babbling, she saw me glance at the marks on her wrists. The ice broken, I now sensed warmer waters between us. But that didn't stop my surprise when she openly started telling me about *her* life.

"My parents are divorced, too, and my dad, who I was so close to, moved across the country. I live with my mom. She's always busy. She never has time for me. I feel like I'm always waiting for something, waiting for my father to come visit, waiting for my mom to give me some of her attention, waiting for my teachers to see that I am actually smart, even though I couldn't care less about geometry because it's boring and useless, and waiting for the boy I like to finally notice me . . . to notice I'm alive, to see me, I guess." As she spoke on and on, I listened.

When she finally finished, I asked her if she had talked to her mom and dad and told them how she felt and what her needs were. Blaire said she felt uncomfortable doing so. I mentioned that sometimes it's okay to feel uncomfortable, but don't let it stop you from taking a risk. If your parents don't know what you're going through, they won't know to be any different. Maybe they need help helping you. She nodded in agreement and then glanced at the book in my hand. I wondered if it was the animated cover with the well-beloved bear that caught her attention. "Is it good?" she asked. I told her, "I think so. I've read it many times. I know the cover looks like a kid's book, but it's actually for adults." She continued to talk. I continued to listen.

Before I knew it, it was time to pick up my daughter at school. I told Blaire it was great meeting her and passed her the book still lodged in the palm of my right hand, *The Tao of Pooh*. She took it graciously. "Thank you," she said with a look of surprise. I smiled wide. I told her that my number was written on the inside cover and that if she ever felt like talking, to give me a call or text. She thanked me again and I got up, readying myself to go.

As I walked away, I turned back to her and said, "You can't fit a square peg in a round hole."

"What?" she asked.

"You'll see."

A few months later, I received a text from Blaire. She told me that since our talk and reading *The Tao of Pooh*, she eventually got the courage to talk to both of her parents, and they *heard* her. And that she hadn't cut herself since. Sometimes, all it takes is for us to listen so that someone can feel heard.

Your gifts are your superpowers.

SOMEWHERE AND LEX

It's said that when you give someone a gift, and they don't accept it, the gift belongs to you.

I placed the green and blue rainbow-colored hat into my coat pocket, put the leash on my new rescue dog, Window, and headed out the door. It was a frigid January morning. I knew on this cold day, well below freezing, I would find someone who needed a soft and very warm hat. With each purchase, the company that made the hat donates and feeds five meals to a hungry child . . . a gift already. With the ease of online purchasing, it's nice at times to be mindful and intentional about where our money goes. The money we spend can get us what we want while also giving back.

Today, as Window and I strolled down Lexington Avenue, I saw a man sitting on the freezing sidewalk, leaning his back against the grey brick wall that surrounded Petco. He wore only pants and a jacket, no gloves or hat to protect his bald head. Being exposed to the wind and chill like that must have made him feel even colder. I walked over to him, smiled as I looked down into his warm amber eyes, and asked, "Do you need a hat?" He nodded. I pulled out the rainbow hat from my pocket, took off my gloves, and gladly gave him all three. He looked up at me with a big grin and said, "God bless you." I smiled again and continued my journey down Lexington Avenue.

Whoever said small things don't make a difference

has never slept in a tent with a mosquito.

THE GIRL IN THE DELI

I was in the local deli one day, eager to place an order. I was craving pickled herring in cream sauce, a favorite of my mom's that always lovingly reminds me of her. There was a long counter where the food was gloriously displayed, which of course tantalized my hunger even more. A smaller one stood perpendicular to it, filled with tiny items they tried to tempt you with while waiting to pay. Small chocolates, violet mints, and Beeman's gum . . . yum.

While waiting for my turn to order, I heard a man's loud voice and then a soft, pleading voice behind me say, "Dad, please stop." I turned to see where the voices were coming from and saw a man standing between two teenage girls. They were only a few feet away from me. A sweet-looking girl, maybe fourteen years old, was the one talking and standing to his left. She had straight blond hair the thickness of a horse's mane and lovely, sad blue eyes. On the other side of him stood another girl with the same blond hair and similar blue eyes, except *sans* the sadness. She was taller, and I sensed she was the other girl's older sister.

Then I heard it again, a soft voice begging, "Dad, please stop. Just please stop." He didn't. He kept berating the younger girl, criticizing her for the way she played in her game on that cold morning. I knew right away they were talking about hockey. I was familiar with the game because I once dated and then married (husband number one) a Boston University hockey player.

On and on her father went, relentlessly brutal. He only stopped for a second when his older daughter interjected, "Dad, enough already!" He turned to her and nastily shouted, "You be quiet—I'm not talking to you!" She retracted like a wounded animal hit by an arrow and didn't say another word. He seemed to have the talent of shooting her down with a painfully sharp arrow. He proceeded to go on and on, demeaning his younger daughter. He was cruel. It seemed to continue forever.

I couldn't help but turn to look at the young girl. I noticed tears about to overflow in her eyes; they revealed so much. She again pleaded, "Please, please stop. I'm begging you to stop." Her voice was so small, so weak. I could barely hear her. But I did. She just couldn't take it anymore. I couldn't either.

I turned around and walked over to them, never making eye contact with the father, who stood to my left, or his other daughter to my right. I gave my attention only to her, the small, fragile girl with pain in her eyes. I smiled as I stared directly into her glassy blues and said, "Oh, you're talking about hockey, right?" She nodded her head. I went on excitedly, "I thought so; I'm very into hockey. My friends played on the U.S. Olympic hockey team that won the gold medal." I jokingly added, "Well, that tells you how old I am."

These were COVID-19 days and she was wearing a mask, so I didn't see if she was able to crack a smile. I leaned in toward the young girl, my upper body bending right in front of her father like he was invisible.

Her eyes locked on mine, she pleaded with me to stay (I'm fluent in eye language), so I firmly said, "He's telling you everything you did wrong now, but when you get home, he's going to tell you everything you did right." I stretched my arm and made a fist that went right past her father to fist bump her. She ever so slowly, ever so weakly, raised her limp arm toward mine as if she were lying in a hospital bed. He seemed to have sucked the life out of her. She continued raising her arm until our fists finally touched.

We stood still like that for a moment, our gaze fixed on each other. No words were necessary. I felt her pain. I also felt her gratitude for the brief reprieve the encounter brought her. I turned and walked back to my place in line at the food counter. He never spoke another word.

It doesn't take much to make someone else's day.

COMPLIMENTS OF
THE HOUSE

My husband, Bobby, and I were in the local Starbucks recently when I noticed a girl about sixteen years old behind the counter filling orders. The small, soft features of her face were nearly taken over by the large, silver railroad-track braces that lined her teeth. She had such a pleasant disposition. She looked like she was twelve years old—her appearance and demeanor reminded me of a daisy or peony not yet in full bloom. I noticed how pretty the front pieces of her shoulder-length light brown hair looked, dyed a fuchsia-like pink. I told her I really liked her hair. Her tiny round face lit up like a bright full moon. A few minutes later, I heard my name called as she appeared again, placing my decaf cappuccino and my husband's café mocha on the counter. I thanked her, and as we left, I glanced back once more before reaching the door. The girl was still looking in my direction, and our eyes met. With an endearing smile, she waved and said, "Have a nice day!" I wished her the same as I pushed open the door.

Once outside, my husband asked, "Do you really like her hair?" I remember thinking, *how cynical.*

"Yes, I do," I said. "Why do you ask?"

He pressed on, "Really?"

"Yes," I repeated and added that I felt she might like to hear something nice today. My husband responded, "I knew it! I knew you didn't really like it; you just wanted to pay her a compliment." I guess he was half right. I did want to pay her a compliment and thought it would make her feel good, but only because I *meant* it. I liked her hair—on her. Did it bother him that he didn't like it and wanted me not to like it? What did he mean by like? Maybe our versions of the word were different.

Upon pondering these questions, I came to the realization that what I mean by the word "like" could very well be quite different from his. I *liked* that this young woman took the time to find her individuality, and I identify with that. I also *liked* honoring that in her. I *liked* saying something nice that made her happy. It was spontaneous and authentic, which is probably why she appreciated it so much. I liked the whole interaction. While her hair may not be right for me, that didn't mean I couldn't appreciate it on someone else. It looked great on her. And I loved telling her so.

My friend Ana and I were recently on the phone having one of our usual insightful conversations. Being two talkers, it wasn't unusual for us to end up chatting for hours. That day, she told me she was bothered because she couldn't remember things she recently read. They were nonfiction books on Buddhism, meditation, and other topics that were totally of interest to her, which is what surprised and frustrated her. I heard the disappointment in her voice. "So many books," she said. "So many highlights, and I can't repeat a thing."

I told her not to worry because there are those who can reiterate things word for word. They communicate exactly that, no more, no less. And then there are those who become changed by what they read. They live it. That's their way of sharing with the world what they've learned. They show others by example. I told her that's what she does. I felt her smile through the phone.

Never undervalue the power of kindness.

FOREIGNERS IN A FOREIGN LAND

On a recent trip to Portugal, my friend Ana and I decided to take a day trip from Lisbon, which we both loved, to nearby Sintra. Our centrally located boutique hotel in Lisbon, tastefully decorated in soft pastel hues, was the perfect starting point for any adventure around the city and beyond. The person behind the desk recommended a tour company they always used, so we booked them for the next day.

We were the first ones picked up the next morning by our tour guide, Noah. A twenty-eight-year-old with a thick head of hair and a full, light-brown beard, he reminded me of a young rabbi I'd once known. Noah lived with his girlfriend and their two young children. We stepped into his oversized white van with me in front next to him and Ana on the bench seat right behind him. Next, we picked up two more travelers from Ireland who introduced themselves as Ashley and her son, Alan, who looked to be in his early thirties. Ashley got in first and sandwiched herself between Ana and her son. She wore a printed white skirt with small peach flowers that came down to her knees and a peach, short-sleeve cotton top. I remember her clothing because it was very 1950s retro. We then gathered the last two tourists, a husband and wife who sat in the last row, and with all six of us buckled up, the adventure began.

We quickly came to appreciate Noah for being so knowledgeable and personable. You could tell he loved his work. On the way to the National Palace of Pena, considered one of the most prized attractions in Portugal, I took in the green surroundings that passed me by and noticed the many different trees. They seemed misplaced or something—they didn't look native—so I asked the informed Noah. He explained to us that those trees were indeed not native to Portugal but imported from all over the world by King Ferdinand II in the 1800s as part of his restoration of the palace and its grounds. With his vivid, Romantic-era imagination, the king wanted Pena Park to be a magical forest surrounding the castle. And magical it was! At one point, I opened my window and smelled a familiar scent I had loved but couldn't place. I asked my fellow travelers if they smelled it and knew what it was, and Noah replied that it was rosemary. He said it was not the kind we eat but a variety that grows wild in the area and is much larger.

During the tour of the palace, Ashley and I walked to-gether and talked. She said something that made me laugh, so I told her I thought she was funny. "No, I am not funny," she insisted. "I am not funny." Her seriousness made me leave it at that. A bit later, when she and I were waiting in line outside the ladies' room, she leaned her back against the wall and told me that her life was very hard. I said, "Oh, because of Alan?" as I nodded toward him. Her son was never too far away from her.

"I'm surprised you didn't know my son is autistic," she said. I told her I detected something but wasn't sure exactly what it was. Ashley explained that her son was severely autistic. Her mom, who had helped out and taken care of him while she was at work, had recently passed, so now her dad, who has some health issues himself, helped out. She then revealed to me that she herself was mildly autistic and continued telling me about her difficulties. I listened. I told her it was nice that at least she and her son could go on vacation together and then offered her to go first when an empty bathroom stall became available.

The day ended with all smiles as we headed toward the van that was to take us back to Lisbon.

Noah first dropped off the couple who sat in the far back and then stopped at Ashley and Alan's hotel. When they were about to get out of the back seat, I said goodbye to both and turned to Alan and asked him if he had a good time. He responded yes without looking at me and walked toward the hotel entrance. Ashley exited the van next and, instead of walking straight to the hotel, came and stood by my open window, her arms taut, hanging straight by her sides. She stood there expressionless, staring down at me without speaking a word. I told her it was great meeting her. She didn't budge but continued standing stiff as a Buckingham Palace guard. Not knowing what to do or what she wanted, I instinctively reached out the window and gave her rigid body a big hug. When I let go, I thought I saw a slight smile appear on her face. Then, without a word, she turned around and walked toward her hotel.

After I arrived home, I shared the story with my daughter. She said, "Mom, you're lucky. You're not supposed to just grab and hug someone without their permission!" I told her I was just following my intuition and felt that that was what Ashley wanted, but didn't know how to ask for it.

Before, during, and after that meeting with Ashley and her son, I've tried to keep kindness as my default in almost any situation. It never lets me down.

PART IV

GRATITUDE

Gratitude is the rebel against

any emotion that holds you back

from experiencing joy.

The secret to having it all . . .

is believing you already do.

RUBY-THROATED WONDER

One evening, the most beautiful thing happened. Up front in the passenger seat of my bright red Chevy Suburban, I was enjoying the drive to my log cabin house in the Catskills, the mountains in Upstate New York that offer breathtaking vistas, hiking trails, waterfalls, and forest preserves. During the ride, my mind drifted through memories of seeing my friend, a ruby-throated hummingbird, at our sanctuary on the mountain. Hummingbirds are my favorite birds. They are known to pick their best-loved places and visit the same ones year after year. They're smart and remember every flower that feeds them. I always looked forward to their visit. This one (and I have had many over the years) had been coming every spring through summer for the past four years. Like the ones before him, he would hover right in front of me, gracing me with his presence as I sat on the front porch. He'd linger for a few seconds and then dart away. Every time, I felt like he knew me.

I once read that hummingbirds have over nine hundred feathers, and trying to imagine how small those were on my little friend made me smile as we drove along. This was the first time in fourteen years I'd been away from the cabin for a span of a few months. COVID-19 had me stationed in one place. I wasn't able to plant the multicolored cosmos like I did every year, the flowers that nourish him, the ones he loves to taste with his quick tongue. I knew I'd have to wait a while before seeing him and felt saddened that he may not come at all. I was worried about him. If he did return, what would he eat? Sure, there were wildflowers all around, but I knew he really loved my daisy-like pink, white, and fuscia cosmos.

As we pulled up to the cabin, I noticed how tall the grass had grown, so wispy and beautiful, at least a couple of feet high, taller than I had ever seen it. I had never seen my home entirely engulfed by the tall green blades and lovely pastel wildflowers that surrounded it. I looked forward to taking a video of this eye-nurturing site from the house as soon as I settled in because the swaying, thirty-inch towering blades of grass were to be mowed the next morning.

After finally stepping onto the porch and starting to film from my phone, I was startled by a loud yet familiar helicopter-type noise. Although I knew that sound, I was so focused on my iPhone that I jumped back and screamed before realizing it was my faithful friend, the hummingbird. No wonder they're nicknamed hummers. He had come to say hello.

I thought I may have frightened him away by my outburst, but when I played back the video, there he was, hovering right in front of me. He had been there long enough to be captured in my video forever. I felt blessed that he showered me with his presence yet again.

As I looked out over the view of the setting sun, I thanked all the hummingbirds in the world for teaching us to be wise like them. To drink the sweet nectar of our own lives.

When we have gratitude, at the bottom of everything, there's always a hallelujah.

A DOUBLE SHOT OF GRATITUDE

A friend of mine was telling me a story as we sat in a coffee house on the Upper East Side where we both lived. While sipping our espressos, she described an encounter she had at the supermarket the day before. While waiting in line, the guy in front of her started to speak to her. After chatting about the usual things people who don't know each other talk about, he mentioned how beautiful she was and asked if she'd like to have dinner with him one night. As I sat across the table listening to her, her tone threw me. *Why is she so annoyed?* Her next words made it clear. "Ugh," she said, "if that's all I can get is some loser who isn't even good-looking, waiting in line at the grocery store, forget it! I give up." She was visibly angry.

I leaned toward her in disbelief and told her I saw the whole episode from a totally different point of view. "How about looking at it like this," I suggested. "Instead of the self-talk you just shared with me, say to yourself, 'Wow, isn't that nice? Today, a friendly person started talking to me while I was waiting in line to buy groceries. He told me I was beautiful. Such a sweet thing to hear.'" I told her that if she looked at the encounter in another way, with an open mind and heart, her annoyance would turn into gratitude. She could see it as it truly was, a gift. Her disappointment over the whole scenario could dissolve into joy like the two sugars in her coffee.

A few months after that incident, my friend called, all cheerful. She told me she had been checking out some books at the library when she met a nice man who told her she had pretty eyes. This time, she didn't throw the gift away. Instead, she felt grateful.

In the midst of chaos, be still.

EVERYTHING'S OKAY.
REALLY.

While working for the wilderness program for troubled teens and young adults in Montana in the late 1980s, I lived in a very small town in the northwest corner of the state. The town had a population of about 600 and looked like the set of an old Western with one gas station and one bar. That was it. To buy groceries or anything else, you had to drive twenty-one miles to the nearest town of Kalispell. Glacier National Park was further away, about an hour's drive, and I got to know that route well because I spent most of my time there for work and my time off. Glacier's dramatic, alluring mountains, along with its running waterfalls, inviting lakes, and epic hikes, were an explorer's dream. It certainly was mine.

The house, well, actually, the *cabin* I rented in the little town, was set on Little Bitterroot Lake. It was a cozy little two-bedroom home with a wood stove and large windows in the living room that gave us a magnificent view of the blue, pristine lake. I shared the place with a guy I didn't know but who worked in the same wilderness program and also needed a place to live. The arrangement worked out well for both of us. Mike had one dog, and I had two, so when one of us was out on an extended wilderness trip, the other, who worked at the center only a few miles away, cared for all the dogs.

I adored that cabin. I would wake up early and, with coffee in hand, gaze out the window at the blanket of fog that hid the lake. I loved watching the mist slowly lift to reveal the water like a lover cautiously pulling off the blanket to uncover the beautiful bare body underneath. It was like waking up with one love and then spending the day with another.

One chilly morning, when I was getting ready to make the drive to Kalispell, the thermometer outside the window read about fourteen degrees Fahrenheit. The grey, cloudy sky covering made it feel even more frigid. I pulled on my hat and gloves and brought my neighbor's television, which was sitting just inside the front door, to my car. They needed it fixed in town, and I volunteered to take it. That's how it was around there; we always tried to save somebody a trip to town. The route was a straight shot down a two-lane highway, and I always enjoyed the picturesque, peaceful ride. That morning showed no sign of snowfall, and the roads seemed to be clear. Or so I thought.

I jumped into my bright orange-red Chevy Blazer, and everything was fine for the first few miles. Then, I started to skid on what must have been black ice. I had never heard of black ice, but I found myself moving in slow motion for what felt like an eternity. My SUV slid into the oncoming lane, and an enormous logging truck was coming straight at me. At the last second—and I have no idea how—my little SUV slid right in front of the giant truck and passed clear of it by a hair. My Blazer rambled down a small grassy bank on the other side of the road and came to a gentle stop at a telephone post. I wasn't hurt at all, just shaken and totally in awe. The first thought that popped into my head was, *The universe has my back.*

That was 1988. I believed it then, and I still believe it today.

PART V

BEEN HERE BEFORE

Life after life, I

become a combination

of all I have ever been.

Some of our oldest memories may

be older than we are.

MAPPED OUT

When I was twenty-two years old, I married my college sweetheart in the month of May. Tony was a Boston University hockey player and eventually the captain of the team. I'll never forget the thrill of watching him play in the Beanpot games, the annual tournaments for the area's four big college rivals —Boston University, Boston College, Harvard University, and Northeastern University. To this day, good old BU still holds the record for the most wins for the men's championship. Go Terriers!

Tony and I met through one of my good friends who had a massive crush on one of Tony's good friends, who was also a hockey player. My friend constantly dragged me to the Dugout, a bar where all the hockey players hung out. She didn't have to drag me far since I lived in the apartments above the place. Tony was a bartender there. His boyish good looks drew me in like a magnet to a goal net.

We fell madly in love, and with him being Canadian and me American, the only way for us to be together (and we couldn't stand being apart) was to get married.

And that we did.

We had a beautiful wedding at the Carlyle, a luxurious yet charming hotel on the Upper East Side of Manhattan where the celebrated cabaret singer and pianist Bobby Short often played, and A-list celebrities regularly checked in. Jacqueline Kennedy Onassis and Audrey Hepburn first met at the Carlyle, and the likes of David Bowie, Neil Young, Hunter Thompson, and Andy Warhol considered it cool. So did I.

Since our jobs kept us from taking a honeymoon right away, Tony and I didn't leave for London and Paris until six months later. This was our first time visiting anywhere in Europe, and we loved it. Many memories remain from that trip, but two stand out. While in London, my new husband stood in Trafalgar Square wearing his Colombo-style khaki raincoat, arms stretched out with swarms of pigeons landing on him. What a sight! He wanted me to join him, but I cringed, thinking it might turn into a scene from Alfred Hitchock's *The Birds*. Fearless Tony, on the other hand, smiled and laughed through the whole thing.

In Paris, the beauty and romance at every turn was overwhelming. We couldn't get enough of it, or each other. I loved so much of the City of Light, especially Montmartre.

I felt something special there that stayed with me—I believe the artistic vibes ignited the creativity that would eventually surface in me years later. But at the time, I had no idea what was to come. Me, a painter? What? Before and after that inspiring trip, I always got in trouble for coloring outside the lines. I still do.

During our five-day stay, Tony and I walked everywhere to take in as much of Paris as possible. My new spouse was in charge of the map, the folded paper kind that somehow managed to keep centuries of humanity on track until Google Maps came along. We stayed at a small hotel on the Left Bank, dimly lit, quaint, and inviting. We loved visiting the charming Market Street on Rue Cler in the seventh arrondissement, renowned for its cobblestones, colorful displays of fresh flowers, and lovely food shops.

On the morning we were to visit Notre-Dame, the cathedral that dates back to 1163, I woke up excited to see the magnificent medieval church, one of the most famous in the world. I love basking in the energy of all worship sites—there's magic there. No matter the religion, one can always feel the unique energy in those places, like being blessed by something greater than ourselves. After our usual morning meal of *deux cafés et croissants* at our favorite spot near the hotel, we started on our journey. While walking, talking, and taking in all our surroundings, we got lost in time and space, and when Tony reached into his pockets to draw out the map, he found them empty. We stared at each other momentarily, and I suddenly blurted, "Don't worry—follow me."

I started walking, my internal compass directing me. Tony joined me without question, probably thinking it was another of my crazy detours. We walked and walked until we found ourselves standing right in front of the glorious cathedral. My husband was in awe, not just from the sight before him but also from the fact that I, alone, without a map, got us there. He turned to me, shocked, and asked how I did it. My answer, which came out of nowhere, surprised us both.

"I don't know. I just feel like I've been here before."

Parts of Paris felt like home to me, as intimately familiar as sections of Boston or Manhattan. That experience led me to research reincarnation, something I'd heard about but never really understood.

After Paris, I did.

Wisdom has no age requirements.

A SONG IN THE
POOL HOUSE

One day, when our daughter, Montana, was about three years old, Judd and I were upstate at our mountain retreat in the Catskills, also known as the Catskill Forest Preserve. Much of the area is state land that can't be developed, and the trees, flowers, birds, and butterflies were truly a treasure for our senses. Our home was on top of East Mountain, which overlooked the many other mountain ranges visible in the distance. On this warm sunny day, we wanted to go swimming. Judd was on the tractor moving some large stones and would meet us when he was finished. As Montana and I changed into our bathing suits, she happily sang a song she made up. I was a bit distracted, busy tidying up and putting our clothes into the lockers in the pool house. (I'd had the white lockers installed to mimic the ones we had at school when I was a kid.) Not until I finished placing

Montana's lilac bike shorts and daisy-flowered T-shirt in the lockers did I finally hear her words: "And God sends everyone back to life." How odd. Since neither Judd nor I were very religious, and I don't remember even using the word "God" in her presence, I thought it was interesting for her to sing something like that. I had never heard the word "God" come out of her mouth before. So I turned to her and asked what she thought "God" meant. She said, "I don't know, Mama, what does it mean?"

"Well, you said it, so what do you think it means?"

She stood still for a moment, and I could tell her beautiful little brain was churning. She then exclaimed, "Oh, I know, Mama—God is love."

Wow.

Her words about God bringing people back to life reminded me of my belief in reincarnation based on my own experiences. Sometimes I had doubts, but Montana's song swept them away. For instance, when Montana was born, the second the nurse put her in my arms, I knew her. I recognized her instantly, as if all our lives together flashed before me all at once. *Oh, my God, she's back*, I said to myself. I was overwhelmed with the connection that was as real as her heartbeat.

If you feel like you've been here before,

maybe you have.

SHE KEPT ME WARM

We lived in California for a few months while Judd was in the large ensemble cast of stars filming the sci-fi action film *Independence Day*. We rented a quaint little house in Beverly Hills. My mom had already moved to Los Angeles because the warmer weather was better for her rheumatoid arthritis. One day, when Judd was on a shoot, my mom came over, and we took my three-year-old girl, Montana, to the neighborhood playground. We had a great time pushing her on the swings, watching her run around, glide down the slides, and try to climb the short ropes.

We soon got thirsty in the city heat and made our way to the drinking fountain. Montana ran ahead and stood before the fountain but couldn't reach the water, even standing on her tippy toes. My mom and I watched as she stuck out her tongue to catch the water but never got close enough. She kept trying and trying, never reaching a drop. With a frustration I had never witnessed in her before, she made two fists and flung her tiny arms down to her sides and announced loudly, "Ugh! I am so frustrated—I can't do anything. I can't even reach the water fountain because I'm stuck in this three-year-old body!"

Whoa! My mother and I stood there speechless. In the past, Montana had mentioned things to me about her other lives, but it had been a while. I calmly stepped over, picked her up, and held her over the fountain so she could get a drink. As soon as she was done, I placed her down and off she went to play as if nothing had happened.

One or two years later, when Judd, Montana, and I were lying in bed watching TV, I gazed at my little girl and said, "I'm cold, and it's so strange because before I had you, I was always hot." She thought for a moment and then said, "I know why, Mommy. I know why. Because my soul was always inside of you, and that kept you warm, but then I came out, and you got cold."

~⁊

Six years earlier, when Judd and I were spending a month traveling in France, Italy, and Switzerland for our honeymoon, we were having dinner at Joe Allen, the oldest (yet still relatively new) American restaurant in Paris. Judd felt more in his comfort zone eating at a place with the same name and owners as the Joe Allen we often frequented in the Theater District in our own city of Manhattan. The place in New York was like a second home to us. The décor of this restaurant in Paris was different, though, nothing like the two dark rooms where one might find themself sitting at a corner table for a brief conversation over drinks with Al Pacino, as Judd and I did one evening. No, this Joe Allen was white and light and just one big airy room . . . sans the Broadway stars.

I remember what I wore that evening thirty-one years ago and still have that very dress. I still wear it—a long, sheer, flowy, burgundy dress with small, subtle, neutral-colored flowers. I needed to wear something underneath because of the transparency of it all, so I also wore a tight-fitting, cream-colored bodysuit. I still have that, too. The Paris restaurant was crowded, as if they were giving something away, and half the city wanted a chance at it. As they sat us down, I couldn't help but notice the beautiful little girl sitting at the next table. Her long, silky black hair reminded me of a Gypsy horse's mane, and her large, dark brown eyes, the shape and size of two enormous almonds, were glued onto mine. I couldn't escape her gaze, and I didn't want to. I could see her mother out of the corner of my right eye as their table was positioned at a thirty-degree angle to ours. They were speaking French, and I understood none of it. Suddenly, the little girl got up from her table, came over to me, and gently began touching my hair. She ran her small fingers down the sleeve of my dress from my shoulder to my hand. Me being me, I wasn't bothered or shocked by her behavior; in fact, I felt the opposite since she seemed somewhat familiar to me.

The little angel jumped into my lap and started stroking my brown curly hair, which fell just below my shoulders. As she did that, she kept looking at me and telling me she loved me in French: "Je t'aime, je t'aime." I did understand those words—I once dated a Frenchman, after all—but even more, I *felt* her. I recognized the universal language of love in her. Her parents, who spoke some English, kept apologizing for their little girl's behavior and called her back to their table. She wouldn't budge. This magnificent creature sitting on my lap and hugging me continued to express her love to a complete stranger. But was I really a stranger?

When their food arrived, her parents called her over again, and she coasted back to her table to eat. While Judd and I glanced at our menus, which were written in both French and English, they told us that it was entirely out of character for their little girl to do something like that because she was always so shy. Their son, who was home not feeling well, was the outgoing one. When the three of them finished their meal and were about to leave, the girl returned to me. She threw her arms around my neck, said one more "Je t'aime," and kept kissing me on my cheek. I kissed her back on hers.

After they left, I wondered why I felt I knew her. Did I know her in another life? Does she look like someone I know now? I turned to Judd and asked, "Does she look familiar to you?" The look on his face told me he was visibly uncomfortable with the whole encounter. "No," he said. "She probably just looks like an actress we know."

"I don't know any actresses who are nine," I said, and left it at that.

When Judd and I lived in the West Village in New York City, we sometimes took Montana, who was two years old at the time, to a local coffee house where each of us had scrambled eggs and well-done toast for breakfast. Then, the three of us would head to the neighborhood playground she loved. We placed her in a black rubber toddler swing, and Judd went behind her to push while I stood before her, grabbing her feet as she came close and then releasing them. All three of us were laughing and having fun when suddenly Montana pointed at me and said in a very serious voice, "Hi, Mommy—I remember you; do you remember me? I was you, and you were me." *Hmm, interesting*, I thought. *Could she have been my mother in a past life?* She didn't stop there, though. Judd and I decided to switch positions, he moving up front and playfully grabbing her feet, bringing them a little higher, and then letting go. Such joy. What better sound than a child's laughter? Then again, Montana got serious, but this time pointed to Judd and said, "And he's my second daddy."

After Montana said this, with my sense that Montana and I already knew each other from a past life or many past lives, I thought she might be referring to having a different father in a previous life. Maybe this *was* a first for she and Judd.

Another time, when Montana was a bit older, she and I were watching a VHS tape of the original animated movie *Snow White*. A few moments into the film, she blurted out, "Mommy, remember when I was big, and you were little, and I used to hold Granddaddy's hand, and we wheeled you in a carriage?" Carriage? Where did she get that word? She only knew the word "stroller." I never wanted to inhibit her, so I gently said, "I'm not sure I remember; I was so little. I was just a baby."

I know Montana and I have been together in other lifetimes, and not just because she announced it when she was very little. The first time I was alone with Judd on a date at his upstate house, when I still barely knew him, I told him over a game of pool that we would get married and have a little girl. He looked at me like I was crazy. I lost the pool game, but won the prize. She came back.

Montana's past-life tidbits have always fascinated me, but some of my encounters with past-life memories have been far less charming.

~ঌ

One evening, I took a friend to a private screening at the Paris Theater across the street from the Plaza Hotel. Being married to a celebrity certainly had its perks—Judd received many such invitations. That particular evening, he was working out of town, so I took a girlfriend. The Paris Theater, with its dramatic purple velvet curtain, is one of my favorites. The only single-screen movie theater left in New York City, it opened in 1948, and Marlene Dietrich cut the ribbon on opening night.

As we entered the theater to make our way to the red velvet seats, an usher handed each guest a complimentary bag of popcorn and a bottle of water. We settled in and enjoyed the show.

I was a smoker back then, so as soon as the movie finished, I hurried outside to light one up. While smoking and chatting about the movie with my friend, a guy came over and asked me if I had an extra cigarette. I didn't think twice and pulled a pack of American Spirit yellows from my purse. As I handed him one, I looked at his face for the first time. Shivers ran up my spine as he asked me for a light. I lit his cigarette and said, "I know you. Maybe you've worked on one of my husband's films or TV shows or something. Do you know me?"

"I know you, too," he said, "but not from that. I'm from South Africa, and I only arrived in the United States last night. I've never been to the U.S. before." An eerie feeling came over me, and a ball of fright burned in my stomach. I grabbed my friend's arm and pulled her toward the street to look for a taxi. We waved one down, and once inside, I told her that I not only knew that man but had an unshakable feeling that he harmed me in another life.

Maybe he remembered, too. Why else would he say he knew me?

PART VI

HEAL

Energy gives life—and healing—

to the body.

The doors to higher consciousness are open.

Feel free to enter.

JUST IMAGINE

The power to heal oneself can be extraordinary. When I was in my late twenties, I developed an enormous and very painful abscess in my throat about once a year. I couldn't eat solid food, only liquids, as I tried to muster the courage to swallow. Delirious with pain and desperate to alleviate it, I decided to do something I had never done before. I decided to try to heal myself.

To this day, I'm not sure how I discovered this method or how it came to me. All I know is that I was desperate to try anything that could grant me some relief. So, as I lay in my bed, I closed my eyes. I imagined I was walking up a path through a forest of spruce trees. A splash of red maples outlined my view like a pencil outlining an image on a page for a child to color. Up and up I went until I couldn't ascend any further. I came to an opening, and there before me was a beautiful swimming hole, quenching its thirst from the runoff of the mountaintop cascading down into its mouth. What a lovely waterfall. The sound was like a soft symphony that soothed my ears as the power of flowing water smoothed out the mountain's jagged edges. The hypnotic sound called to me. I imagined myself standing under this waterfall, the water flowing through my body, washing away the abscess. A steady stream of white light within the water started at my head and then traveled down my throat and out through my feet, carrying my malady with it.

When I awoke the next morning, I could swallow without any pain. I made an appointment to go to my ear, nose, and throat doctor, who was kind enough to fit me in that day. I had been going to him for years, and we knew each other well. To his astonishment and mine, he saw that the abscess was nearly all gone. What usually took at least two weeks of strong medications and agonizing pain only took two days!

Crazily enough, the next time I felt an abscess coming on (I always knew), I did the very same exercises, and it never grew to fruition.

I learned how powerful we really are and that when we're open to possibilities, those possibilities can indeed show up for us. Whether in the form of healing or other ways. This started my thoughts in motion about energy healing.

Years later, when I was in my late forties, I became very sick. I was experiencing extreme stomach pain and acid reflux. I couldn't hold down food. The doctors suggested I eat bland food. I still wasn't getting any better and was losing weight. After many futile tests, no one could figure out what was wrong with me. Sick and discouraged, I forced myself to go on a trip to Los Angeles for my mom's seventy-fifth birthday party that my sister was throwing for her, enduring the journey across planes, trains, and automobiles with my ailing body. I wouldn't miss it for anything. When my sister opened the door, she took one look at me and said with concern, "You should go to a doctor— you look like you're dying!" She's not one to hold back, and her honest words had an enormous effect on my already weak body and mind. I secretly went off to a quiet corner and cried.

The truth is, I thought I was dying, too, so to hear those words felt like a knife piercing through an already fragile heart. After I returned home to New York City, I made a decision. I decided since no one could help me, I would try to heal myself.

I've always been interested in the connection between nutrition and health. A while back, I had stumbled upon a book in my local health food store about the importance of alkalizing your body. I had intuitively bought the book thinking it might help my friend's little girl who had such bad stomach issues that she was in and out of hospitals and could no longer attend school. The doctors couldn't figure out what was wrong with her, so I mailed the book to my friend, hoping it would in some way help her daughter. Little did I know I would need the very same book in the future.

Once back in New York City after my trip to LA, I bought another copy of that book, this time for myself, in an effort to heal whatever was plaguing me. I immediately and drastically changed my diet. I eliminated all gluten and mainly ate (75%) alkaline foods. Within a few months, the pain went away along with my other symptoms. I no longer looked like a skeleton and got back my energy. I felt like myself again. It was astonishing. Truly astonishing!

More recently, just a few years ago, I had a lot of pain in my lower abdomen. I went to my gynecologist, who did a sonogram and told me there was a small mass on the right side of my uterus. She told me more tests were needed to see if it required surgery. I put her off for a few months as I wanted to try to heal myself.

So, I got to it, imagining the waterfall and light just like I did to heal my throat, but with an added step: I made up a mantra for myself. I would say to myself out loud, "Every minute of every day, my uterus is happy and healthy in every way." But I wouldn't just say it. I believed it. I really did.

Two months passed, and I went for the tests my doctor had suggested. When they got the results back, the mass was gone! I had believed—and that belief became my reality!

Times are changing; different healing modalities are becoming available to all of us. The techniques based on *feeling* can sometimes produce instantaneous results, meaning that some of the answers we're seeking actually transcend what's available to us through traditional methods. Someday, who knows, healings we call "miraculous" may instead be recognized as the normal workings of human intention and energy.

We are all a blank canvas—paint your

story any way you'd like.

NOT YOUR USUAL
MARKETPLACE EXCHANGE

Many years ago, I visited Jerusalem, one of the oldest cities in the world, situated in the hills between the Mediterranean and the Dead Sea. I had never been there before, and along with my excitement, I felt the sacredness emanating from the city as soon as I arrived. A transcendent calmness overcame me, unlike anything I had ever felt. I realized then why it is considered a place of divine intervention in our history. A beautiful and magical place, indeed.

I was staying with a friend and her family. Knowing about my intuitive energy healing and ability to read others' energy, they asked me to accompany them to visit one of their friends, a woman in her early forties who, eight months before, had suffered a stroke and couldn't walk. They wanted me to see her and tell them if I thought she would ever walk again. The doctors weren't hopeful. Upon arriving at her large, beautiful, cherry wood–paneled apartment, I was overcome by the heaviness in the air but quickly felt some relief when I eyed a tail-wagging German shepherd lying on the couch. As I walked further into the apartment, about thirty feet away and down a few steps I caught sight of a woman sitting in a wheelchair looking at the computer on her desk. The denseness of the air hit me even harder. A dense aura of negativity surrounded her.

I looked around for my friends, but the two women I came with were already outside on the terrace because they wanted to give us some privacy. The woman looked up at me, and I introduced myself. I wanted to turn and run, but instead, I looked back at the dog, who wagged his tail again when we made eye contact. That calmed me enough to turn my attention back to the lady in the wheelchair. I asked about the events leading up to her stroke. She said it happened when she returned to her hometown for her father's funeral. She then told me all about how her father wasn't very nice to her growing up, that her sister and mother were difficult, to say the least, and that she didn't really have any relationship with them, and her brothers were distant and she had no relationship with them, either, and that she didn't like her job because of her peers.

After ten minutes of listening to her complain, I could tell she was extremely angry and resentful. I turned around and did something I had never done before. I asked her if she wanted to walk again, and when she said yes, I told her the first thing she needed to do was stop playing the victim.

"You're not a victim, Abby. Your thoughts are heavy and dense. When that happens, you vibrate at a lower frequency. When you raise the level of your thoughts to loving, joyful ones, you raise your frequency. That helps you heal. If the lemonade of your life is sour, add sugar before you drink. Don't give all your power to others. Your power belongs to you. And that power will help you get closer to walking again."

She sat silently as I continued, "When we cling to anger or resentment, we only hurt ourselves. As the saying goes, 'Holding onto anger is like drinking poison and waiting for the other person to die.' I think you should go to your physical therapy and change your story, even though that story is all you know. If you feel you can't do it alone, seek out a professional who can help you. The story you keep telling yourself is not working for you. Rewrite another one. It's yours to write."

She turned to face her computer and sat silently for a few moments. When she turned to me again, she said, "Everyone feels bad for me and treats me like a victim, but you don't. No one has ever spoken to me like you just did, pointing out that whatever I'm doing will not help me and that I need to stop playing the victim." Her words shocked me. I had no idea how she would take everything I said, but she seemed to understand.

I went to the terrace to find my friends, and as we headed for the door to leave, I turned around once more and said, "And remember, when we free another, we free ourselves. Bye!" I waved and walked out through the stately mahogany door.

One of my friends stayed with me to introduce me to the Shuk, Jerusalem's popular, partially covered outdoor market with vibrant foods, spices, wines, clothing, and people. By the time we arrived, I had one of the worst headaches of my life. Thinking that maybe some food and drink would help, I suggested we catch a bite before entering to shop. We found a nearby café known for serving the best hummus in town. That it was. I enjoyed a delicious falafel drenched in tahini, a side salad with hummus, and a ton of water, which would usually wash away any headache. This time, it didn't. When we finished lunch and returned to the Shuk, the terrible throbbing in my head persisted. I knew it was from being at that woman's place. I had soaked up a lot of her heavy, negative energy.

I knew I couldn't go on like this, but I had no idea what to do. Before I could give it another thought, my attention shifted to the sound of a baby crying. I spotted nearby a cute, round little boy about seven months old, dressed in a navy-and-white sailor outfit, who was crying and crying, almost screaming. I gazed at his overwhelmed mama, who was trying everything to get him to stop. Nothing was working. Even through his never-ending loud crying, I could feel his sweet energy. I decided to go over to them. The mama, still bent over his stroller, glanced up at me and said, "He's been crying like this for the past thirty minutes, and I can't get him to stop." At that point, I think she would have welcomed any ideas from anyone who showed up. She was completely distressed. I could feel how tense she was; having two children myself, I knew the feeling.

I momentarily turned away from her and started calmly talking to her baby. I kept smiling and talking to him, telling him all about the Shuk and its colorful spices while staring into his big, blue, teary eyes. "Oh, I see you have a nice rattle in your hand," I continued. After a few more minutes of this, he finally stopped crying. I saw the color return instantly to his mama's face. She was so relieved. She wasn't the only one. Right after he stopped crying, my headache disappeared.

Here's the thing. That baby and I had an exchange of energies. Once I connected with him, our link neutralized the dense energy I was carrying around, and my headache was gone. It was a symbiotic exchange. I walked back to my friend, who was standing across the aisle at a vendor displaying brightly colored mounds of spices. Shaking her head at what she had just witnessed, she told me she had watched the energy exchange between me and that baby. "I could feel it from here," she said. "It was amazing."

Many questions entered my mind after that exchange. Was it the Source, a higher power, or God that brought us together for a mutual healing, or was that baby crying on purpose to draw me to him so we could have that mutual exchange? Whatever it was, we are all connected.

We continued roaming through the Shuk, which, even through my daze of astonishment over what had just happened, seemed even more cheerful and bright. Stopping to look through a rack of hand-embroidered blouses, my friend once again shook her head. She laughed and said, "We're going to have a good story to tell our hosts tonight."

"Ha!" was all I could reply.

Connections are ageless.

DANCING IN MYKONOS

My fiftieth birthday was coming up in a few months. I was a divorced mother with two children ages eight and fifteen who lived primarily with me, so when a friend who was also turning fifty called and asked if I'd like to go with her to Greece, a birthday present to ourselves, I thought, *Why not?*

"Where in Greece are you thinking?"

"Mykonos," she said. "Check it out on the internet and let me know what you think."

I looked up my friend's suggestion and couldn't wait for the adventure on that gorgeous island paradise to begin.

Mykonos is pronounced *mee-ko-nos*—even the sound is sexy. My imagination journeyed ahead of me with thoughts of stepping onto the beautiful thirty-three-square-mile island, toes touching the silky, moon-colored sand and the sun wrapping my body in warmth. I wanted more, so

I went to the bookstore the next day and bought a book on the Greek islands. The photos of the quaint white stucco buildings with breathtaking 360-degree views of the ocean were captivating. Mykonos is nicknamed "the island of the winds" because of the strong winds that breathe life across the island, but I think Mykonos is known for much more. The winds were not the only strong presence on the island I would encounter.

We flew nine and a half hours from JFK into Athens International Airport and waited a while before boarding a small propeller plane that took another forty-five minutes to land us on the isle of delights. The hotel was small and charming. Its pristine white steps led us up to our sweet room, where we found two full beds with two simple paintings of iris flowers, likely painted by a local, hanging on the stucco walls above them. I learned that the hotel supported their local artists, a quality I admire. The sliding glass door led us out to a very small terrace with a tiny table and two chairs. Ahh, but the view . . .

The seemingly limitless expanse of the ocean was breathtaking. Everywhere I looked, it was there, like a lifelong friend.

I always travel light with one small, rolling duffel bag. My friend, on the other hand, had four large suitcases suitable for Dwayne "The Rock" Johnson to take on a four-month trip around the world. I gave her a perplexed look.

"I never know what I feel like wearing, so I pack everything I think I might want to wear," she said.

"And all those shoes?"

"To go with the outfits, of course."

My duffel carried one pair of sandals (sexy suede ones); a pair of flip-flops; a fitted, flowery, ankle-length skirt; and just enough casual clothes for five days. I had no problem giving her half of my closet space.

As we walked along the winding, white-washed cobblestone streets the first night, I noticed how pretty the small balconies looked with their overflowing, bright pink flowers. After dinner, I found myself searching for a light for my cigarette. Somewhere deep down, I wondered if that wasn't all I was searching for that night.

Back home I was in an on-again, off-again relationship with a tall, dark-haired musician who captivated me with more than his music, so when I caught sight of a handsome guy smoking, I immediately went over and asked him for a light. He lit my cigarette, as gentlemen do, and I gazed into his large, dark brown eyes. He was with a friend. The four of us started talking together.

The attraction between Andreas and me was instant. My friend started impatiently tapping her foot. Eventually, she ducked into the art gallery near where we stood, and Giovanni, Andreas's friend, followed her inside. Not only was I attracted to Andreas, but my friend seemed to be attracted to Giovanni. Thank God! It appeared the boys felt the same toward us. Perfect. I say "boys" because although they didn't look it in their cool casual clothes and manners, they were twenty years our junior. But that didn't stop us. Or them. My friend with the many clothes chose to lie about her age. I did not.

Andreas asked if we could meet at the beach the next day, but I wanted to spend the days with my friend. So, the four of us made plans to meet in the evenings after dinner. We always split up. Andreas and I wanted to dance the night away. We danced every night until the break of dawn and watched the sunrise over the ocean and he walked me back to my hotel room so I could catch a few hours' sleep. That night, like every night, he took out one of his earbuds, gently placed it in my ear, and played "Thank You" by Dido.

On my last night, we lingered. We wanted to roam the island all night. We didn't sleep. As the sun was about to rise, we stopped by a door that was slightly ajar, sending the aroma of fresh bread wafting out onto the street. I couldn't help but peek in. The owners came out and graciously offered us two French baguettes. That pre-dawn morning, Andreas and I held hands, ate, and shared our bread with the nomadic island cats that greeted us so warmly.

That began my dance with Andreas, which would continue beyond Mykonos.

Once home, I was still in the rocky relationship with my musician. We eventually split up, but a strong connection still exists between us today. It just took a different form. It's like sculpting a mound of Play-Doh in the warmth of your palms—the shape may change, but the original substance is still there.

Being with Andreas had been whimsical, a moment in time that is still etched in my memory. The way he always held my hand. The way we so smoothly danced across the dance floor as if we had been dancing together forever. The way he never let me out of his site, even escorting me to the ladies' room—so protective. I felt like a schoolgirl again.

Two months later, Andreas invited me to his small hometown in Albania, and I gladly accepted. While there, I was introduced to his friendly, lovely family and their close friends and neighbors. They greeted me with such warmth, a melting, delicious warmth like a toasty marshmallow squeezed between two graham crackers. I had never met more welcoming people, and as a big hugger myself, I did not retract or feel uncomfortable when they quickly embraced me upon my arrival. I connected with Andreas's entire family and his neighbors right away.

My favorite neighbor was a fifteen-year-old girl named Drita. She lived with her mama and her dog while her papa lived in Italy, where he worked so he could send money home to them. One day, Drita, who, unlike her mama, spoke English pretty well, invited Andreas and me for tea. We gladly accepted. Upon entering their apartment, Drita flung herself into my arms, shouting, "My mama said God sent you here!" She repeated her words, and I couldn't contain the surprised look on my face. Andreas caught it immediately and came to my side. He took hold of my arm and escorted me to the couch where tea and biscuits were being served on the oval glass coffee table. I looked around and noticed many religious items in the room. I found it hard to grasp what the young girl said, so I thought maybe she meant something different.

Sitting on the couch with Andreas's hand in mine, I was smitten once again as I listened to him tell Drita and her mama the story of how we met on the beautiful island of Mykonos. As Andreas spoke, Drita translated for her mother. I could tell by their smiles that they enjoyed hearing about our chance encounter. When Andreas finished, Drita took her time to speak to us in English about her mother. She told me her mama has only one kidney and that it had been hurting for quite a while, but after I came yesterday and hugged her, her mama said the pain went away. I had no idea what to say to that, so I smiled.

Then, I remembered I had a large bag of unsweetened cranberries in my backpack that I had brought with me from the States because I had kidney stones when I was sixteen and liked to travel with them as a precaution. I went next door to retrieve the cranberries and brought them back to Drita's mom. I told them to buy unsweetened, pure cranberry juice because I knew it was good and cleansing for her kidney. I saw Drita and her mama a few times after that day for tea, and each time was always a special pleasure.

Eventually, my trip to Albania came to an end, along with my dance with Andreas. But something else had just begun.

My interaction with Drita and her mama stirred something inside me. Something I had always known but never really embraced until then. Meeting them marked the beginning of my energy healing adventure.

Since I was a child, I always felt I was put on this Earth to help and heal. Ever since I could remember, people naturally gravitated toward me, their arms stretched out handing me their problems on a silver platter, asking for my help in one way or another, either physical or emotional. One day, when Montana was a little girl and we were at the animal shelter waiting to adopt another dog, she watched as strangers approached me, one by one. "Mommy," she asked, "how come everyone comes to you with their problems?" I told her I didn't know. Eventually, after many years of this and after my trip to Albania, I decided to take it further. I studied to become an energy healer. I'm now a reiki practitioner and master teacher and an intuitive healer.

POWER
TO THE
PEACEFUL

PART VII

CONNECTED

*We are all connected with an
invisible thread that weaves through
the points of all the stars in the sky.*

When we touch someone else's life,

we touch the sky.

SCENE ON A TRAIN

I was on the train, seated by the door where the seats face one another. I always like sitting in that section because it's more airy, and I enjoy the spacious legroom. Across the aisle from me, in the same set of seats, also facing each other, I couldn't help but notice the mother and daughter look-alikes. They both had the same soft, curly, sandy-colored hair. The young girl looked about thirteen years old. She was resting her head against the window, her eyes opening and closing as if she were torn between gazing at the sunset or giving in to her exhausted body. At one point, our eyes caught one another's. We exchanged smiles. I could read her energy; she was more than just tired. She was sick.

I sensed she would recover—the darkness around her was dissipating. For much of the train ride, the sleepy girl opened and closed her eyes like the shutters of a window. When they were open, she would look my way. I'd look back. It was a mutual exchange. It seemed as if we were having a private conversation. We spoke only with our eyes, something I was accustomed to doing with strangers. They are truly the windows to the soul, bringing us far more information about people and the rest of the world than we realize.

It was as if she knew I was sending her healing energy and love. Maybe she could feel it; I don't know.

Eventually, the movement of the train finally lulled her into a pleasant slumber. When her mom—whose name was Sandy, it turns out—was sure her little angel was sound asleep, she started talking to me. Her body language told me she felt comfortable doing so. Something about Sandy was familiar. I couldn't place it at that moment, but after our brief encounter, I realized she reminded me of *me*—we were short women with similar almond-shaped brown eyes, curly hair, and an openness to life. We also seemed to be similar kinds of mommies.

"I could see the connection between you and my daughter, Sophia," Sandy told me. "I saw how she looked at you." She leaned toward me and continued, "My daughter's sick. She has cancer and has been through so much. We're not sure what the outcome will be, but we should know soon. I want to thank you because that's the first smile I've seen on her face in a very long time."

She then told me that they lived in New Zealand and were visiting relatives in the United States, where they were originally from. When she asked if we could exchange phone numbers and emails, I said, "Of course."

We chatted a bit more and I revealed to Sandy that I did energy healing. I thought I saw a guarded sigh of relief. "I believe in that kind of thing," she said. I was elated at her openness and knew that that outlook could only help Sophia. This brought me joy—not everyone is that receptive. I felt excitement throughout my body and had a visceral conviction that Sophia was going to be okay.

When their stop arrived, Sandy stood up and asked if she could hug me. I opened my arms wide and gave her a firm embrace. Then Sophia came over, and we hugged as well. Before sitting down, I glanced down at the length of the car and saw that everyone on the train was staring at us. That came as no surprise. Making a scene was nothing new for me.

I turned to Sophia and said, "You'll be okay. I know it." She smiled again.

Two months later, Sandy called. "I just want to let you know Sophia is cancer-free. She still speaks about meeting you on the train and how when you, a stranger she felt connected to, told her she was going to be okay, she believed you. You gave her hope." She paused for a few seconds and then continued, "Please, if you ever find yourself in New Zealand, give us a call. We'd love to have you over."

My mind raced with her good news, and after thanking her, I thought about how I had always wanted to visit her country. Besides its picturesque beauty, I dreamed of seeing the nation's endangered national bird, the kiwi, in the wild and the white flowers of the Manuka tree that bees forage to produce an exotic honey of the same name. Now, however, I knew those sights would pale in comparison to seeing precious Sophia in the full bloom of health. A natural wonder like no other.

When we judge, we miss the real story.

THE RETROGRADE MOON

That chilly, hazy spring New York City morning, around 6:30 a.m., the sun could barely poke through the thick mist that hung heavily in the morning sky. I was walking my dog on one of the side streets where the trees were already putting on a show, dressed up in bright, bursting foliage. I basked in their way of celebrating the end of winter while giving us the pleasure of their beauty and scents. When Leaf, my long-haired, chocolate-brown rescue who looked more like a bear than a dog, finished saying her hellos to all the neighborhood canines, we happily headed back home. In the distance, I noticed a man who appeared to be talking to himself. I recognized the signs all too well, as I constantly talk to myself to the point where my husband jokingly asks me, "Are you talking to me or your imaginary friend again?" Once I reminded him that at least I was in good company; I heard that Einstein also talked to himself.

The man in the distance was getting closer. He looked a bit disheveled as he looked down, spoke loudly, and waved his arms frantically like he was marching. When he stomped past us, heading in the other direction, I heard him angrily mumbling to himself. Or so I thought. Leaf and I were already near my apartment building when I happened to glance behind my left shoulder. I saw that the man had turned around and was now walking close behind us. He was following me. Holding on to Leaf's leash tighter, I nervously ran back to my building. Once inside, I locked the lobby's front door and started babbling to our doorman about being followed. He peeked through the glass doors to see who I was talking about and said, "Oh, I know him. He delivers the newspapers here." He unlocked the door and returned to his desk.

I was so embarrassed. It was unlike me to quickly judge or feel threatened the way I did. My usual modus operandi is quite the opposite. Before I could mull over that further, the man came into the building and told me he saw me running away from him and didn't know why. I apologized profusely and opened my arms to make room for a hug, which he accepted. We walked out of the building together and began to chat.

He told me his name was Luke. He explained that the moon was in retrograde, which meant we were all going through a bit of a hard time now. It could also be the reason he was agitated on his paper run and why I acted the way I did. I had been combing my mind to find the answer to a problem that weighed heavily on me that morning, and coming up empty. As we shared our stories standing on the sidewalk, this slender, gentle man told me just what I needed to hear. He listened to me with such an open heart. He clasped my hand between both of his and gave me just the advice that meant a lot at that moment—sometimes we're affected by forces we can't see, and sometimes it's easy to jump to conclusions and not see people for who they really are.

Although I tried to live without judging anyone, that day, I deceived myself. I didn't recognize a prince in a Yankees' T-shirt.

The world's beauty is enough.

LIGHTS IN THE SKY

When I was a young woman on my own, I decided to roam across the country solo in my two-door Chevy Blazer I called Bess. My only company would be my dogs, my constant traveling companions. But my plan changed when a good friend begged to join me. She had just gotten married, but she said she'd leave her new husband home if I left my dogs with someone and took her instead. How could I say no to that?

The trip was fabulous! We went to Yellowstone and Jackson Hole. We drove snowmobiles through Grand Teton National Park with its breathtaking views. In Red Lodge, Montana, I fell in love with and bought a Crazy Creek chair, one of the first ever made, a prototype.

While we were driving through Wisconsin one evening around midnight, after being at the wheel for twelve hours, the sky got weird—spectacularly weird. Giant waves of green, white, and pinkish purple danced across the sky as if moving toward us. I pulled over to the shoulder to rest my eyes, figuring they were exhausted, but when I stepped outside and looked up, I saw the gliding, colorful spectacle in full force. *Now I'm really hallucinating*, I thought. We were alone on the dark highway, which added to my rising fear. If my eyes weren't deceiving me, if this was real, was this the end? Was the atmosphere falling apart? Would a trumpet sound next? Did we enter a time-space warp? How would we get back? I woke my friend and nonchalantly asked her to join me in the fresh air. If she didn't see what I saw, I could rest easy about the end of the world, but I'd have to let her drive the rest of the night.

She saw it.

"Whoa," she said quietly, staring at the astonishing play of light above us. Neither of us had seen anything like it before. Once I realized the sky wasn't falling and we were still in Central Time North America, I leaned back and enjoyed the show. It was spectacular.

The next morning, we couldn't stop talking about the wonderous site during breakfast in the motel diner that looked right out of the movie *Bagdad Cafe*. Eggs, toast, coffee, and a lot of excited conversation got us revved up to hit the road. A few minutes into the drive, Bess started to lose her juice. She wouldn't go above thirty miles an hour. I turned around on the still-empty two-lane highway and returned to the diner, where the waitress gave me directions to a car mechanic she knew in the area.

George was a small-framed, handsome older gentleman who, along with his petite and lovely wife, Rose, greeted us warmly. They were special. Their calm, mild manner gave them an aura of steadiness that instantly made me feel that all was right with the world. Dealing with George and Rose wasn't like making a business transaction—it was more like stopping by to connect with family I hadn't seen in years. While George inspected my car, I told him about the strange colored lights in the sky and how it felt like they were flowing down to us as we watched.

"Oh, yeah, the Aurora Borealis," he said without looking up. "We heard they were out last night."

"The what?" I asked.

"The Northern Lights," he said. "They happen when things in the atmosphere hit the magnetic field."

"Particles from the sun," added Rose. "When they hit the atmosphere up north, they light up in color."

I had never heard of the Northern Lights before that day and I have never seen them since. I feel blessed to have witnessed such an extraordinary sight on such an ordinary road.

As my friend and I sat on the curb in the sun, I wondered what other miraculous works of nature were out there waiting to amaze us. The dancing cosmic light show would be hard to top, but who knows?

George fixed my car in a half hour and only charged me ten dollars.

Whispers can be life's secrets revealing

themselves to you.

A FRIEND IS A DOLLAR IN YOUR POCKET

On a cool, brisk day, I popped into one of my favorite convenience stores in Harlem to pick up a bottle of water for the long walk from the train station to my apartment in Carnegie Hill. I admit that on a very rare occasion, I'll buy some kind of lottery ticket, and this time, it was a one-dollar scratch-off that actually paid off.

I liked the vibe in the area and in this small store situated next to the subway, and I always engaged with interesting people on my quick trips in and out. That day, as I entered the store, I happened to turn back and notice the man walking in behind me. He was tall and somewhat regal looking, with smooth tan skin and covered in a long, wool, camel-hair winter overcoat. It reminded me of the one my dad used to wear.

As I turned back to head to the water case, he gently whispered into my ear, "A friend is a dollar in your pocket."

His words were so faint I thought I might have been hearing things, so I faced the stranger. As his warm, intelligent brown eyes looked deeply into mine, he whispered again, "A friend is a dollar in your pocket." I smiled and thought, *Hmm, cool, cool metaphor.*

There was something mysterious about this tall, dark, handsome man, almost as if he were my Clarence, my personal guardian angel, even though I didn't hear any bells ring. It took a second for me to digest his wise words and reply, "I agree." I then went to the familiar face behind the counter, handed him my scratch-off ticket, and with a big, happy grin, said, "Hi! I won fifty dollars!" He moved to another part of the counter, as he always did, to check the ticket. When he returned, he planted his index finger firmly on the receipt and said, "Look—you didn't win fifty dollars; you won a hundred dollars." I was so excited; you'd think I'd won a million! I thanked him for his honesty, paid for my new mysterious friend's coffee and newspaper, and repeated his wise words to them both on my way out: "Yes, a friend sure *is* a dollar in your pocket."

The instantaneous lesson about the interconnectedness of life astounded me, how the universe put those man's wise words into action so quickly. I'm always open, always learning, always amazed.

Synchronicities can occur anywhere, anytime.

COWS, CHOCOLATE,
AND A COWBOY

One beautiful September morning, my husband, Bobby, and I decided to take a drive around nearby Litchfield County, Connecticut. I wanted to visit Arethusa Farm, home to the dairy cows whose pristine and rich milk makes the ice cream the farm is famous for. I had heard that you could meet and greet the cows and learn which one is used for each flavor. Cows and ice cream, two of my favorite things—what more could I ask for?

Cows are such gentle sentient beings. I heard they're fast learners and have the intelligence of a three-year-old child. They have problem-solving skills and experience joy; I love being in their presence.

As for ice cream, I've been known to eat two pints in one sitting. Enough said.

Arethusa Farm was just south of the town of Litchfield and near its dairy plant in Bantam, where the ice cream is made and sold, so we headed to Litchfield first. Upon arriving on the famous Arethusa acreage, we found the fields desolate without a cow in sight. Hoping we'd find them around another corner or hill, we kept driving along the picturesque tree-lined road toward the outbuildings in the distance. As we got closer, we saw that the buildings were barns and all boarded up. The beautiful acres of rolling hills and stunning farmland felt eerie and empty as if the land itself mourned the disappearance of the cows. I couldn't contain my sadness as we left.

Back on the main road, I saw an older woman up ahead standing by her mailbox. She wore faded jeans, a green apron, a sunhat, and gardening gloves. We stopped near her, and I rolled down my window. "What happened to the cows?" I asked. She stepped closer and told us that the owner sold part of the farm to an agricultural society for educational purposes and the cows were sold to someone else. I heard the same regret in her voice that I felt as I listened to the news. Before we drove away, she added that the ice cream place in Bantam was still up and running, and maybe some of the same cows still contributed to it. We decided to first go the other way.

Since it was a hot, late-summer day, I thought an iced coffee would taste good on the drive back, so I suggested we stop in the nearest town. Chocolate sounded good, too. When does chocolate *not* sound good? We explored the next village and found a small, cozy coffee house. After ordering two iced coffees to go, I asked if they sold any chocolate. The woman behind the counter shook her head apologetically and said no. I then heard a man's voice say, "None here, but I know a place that has the best chocolate in Connecticut, and it's real close, too." I turned around, and the man sitting at the closest table grinned at me. He looked right out of an old Western, complete with a white beard and mustache, leather boots, jeans, and cowboy hat. "Thorncrest Farm," he added. "They make it right there."

My mood perked up, and I smiled back. "Oh, really? It's a farm, too? Do they have cows?"

"They sure do, and you can even pet 'em."

"Wow!" I said, using every ounce of control to keep from jumping up and down. The cool cowboy gave us simple directions to the farm and I thanked him many times as I paid for the coffee. Off we went to Thorncrest, just ten minutes north.

The cowboy was right about the chocolate. The sign said it all—Thorncrest Farm & Milk House Chocolates—and the dozen or so cars parked on the side of the road showed it was definitely open for business. The milk house turned out to be a tiny little thing, eight by ten feet at most, with grey barn siding and a charming pane glass door with matching flower boxes just below the sills. It looked more like a kids' playhouse than a chocolate shop, especially from several yards away, where Bobby and I took our place at the end of the long line. The line seemed like too much when all I could think about were the cows, so we headed to the barn.

The cows were ready and waiting for every visitor who walked into the cool, spacious barn that smelled like fresh hay. We walked over to the first stall to see a black-and-white dairy cow who, according to the sign on the stall, was named "A-OK." How appropriate, I thought. She was big, sweet, and friendly and seemed to like it when I ran my fingers along her wide cheeks and above her nose. When another couple stepped over to meet A-OK, we went outside and returned to the line, which was shorter by then.

Inside the little milk house, the scent of warm chocolate was heaven. I bought a few pieces of dark chocolate filled with caramel and sprinkled with sea salt, a couple of dark chocolate truffles, and one milk chocolate heart. They were all delicious, but my favorite was the dark chocolate caramel sea salt. I planned to bring some home, but temptation overcame me and I ate every one of the handmade delicacies right there.

As I licked my fingers during our stroll back to the car, I thought about the series of events that made it possible for me to pet a cow after all. If I hadn't suggested we stop for coffee and we hadn't stopped at that exact place, we wouldn't have learned about the farm. The right information showed up at just the right time. Now that's synchronicity.

On the way home, we had to stop for the famous ice cream in Bantam, too, of course—a perfect ending for an absolutely A-OK-perfect day.

Synchronicities have graced my life for as long as I can remember, including one many years earlier that also involved some coffee klatching.

The summer after my first year of high school, a friend and I went on a cross-country trip organized by Metric Teen Tours. I also went on an eating strike. I came home from that six-week trek weighing only ninety pounds. I learned years later that my condition had a name: anorexia. I recognized the symptoms when I encountered that word, the same symptoms I had endured that summer. I hardly ate, and I lied about it. Nothing could make me want to eat a thing. Luckily for me, I went through this for only a very short time. Not everyone who has the eating disorder has the same fate.

Years later, my close friend Isla, who moved to the United States in her twenties, was visited by her aunt Lucia from Spain. Lucia was in New York to bring her young adult daughter, Martina, to a residential treatment center for eating disorders. The stay was to last at least thirty days. Isla wanted me to meet her aunt so I could share my story, as she knew I had the same disorder when I was a teenager. We decided to meet at our favorite local coffee house, and when I walked in, I found Isla and her aunt seated at a small round table with three chairs. I sat in the empty one. They had just dropped off Martina at the treatment center the day before. I immediately noticed the troubled look on Lucia's face.

After our brief introductions and getting settled in with our cappuccinos, the conversation turned to the topic of the hour. I discussed what I thought brought about my experience with anorexia and made sure to be clear that there are different reasons for different people. Looking back, I explained, I believed mine may have been caused by a sense of a lack of control and having to grow up too fast. By that summer, everything in my life had changed all at once: my parents got divorced, my first love and I broke up, and my older sister left for college. I didn't know anyone at the time whose parents were divorced, and I felt like I was losing everyone. "I was only fifteen years old," I said, "and all that change was scary. I was overwhelmed."

I then talked about how important it is in general for any of us to feel empowered and how that could certainly help with anorexia as well as other disorders. After I said this, out of the corner of my eye, I saw a beautiful young girl at the next table smile at me, and I smiled back. Our tables were so close I was sure she had heard our conversation, and she confirmed that by looking at me with her eyes wide open and saying, "I love this conversation!" She jumped right in and continued, "Yes, I agree. It's so important to feel empowered, and that was my favorite class." Hmm, I thought to myself, how interesting and wonderful that this girl, for some reason, took an empowerment class. Very progressive. She then mentioned that she took the class when she was in treatment. Another hmm.

This kind of chatting between us went on for about an hour. I loved every time she boldly joined our conversation. She was so full of life and joy as she told us about starting college in the fall and how excited she was for her new adventure to begin. The three of us enjoyed her conversing with us very much. Finally, I decided to be bold myself and ask her what she was in treatment for. She answered, "Anorexia." Her personality was warm, open, and energized as she shared her story with us. Wow, I thought—I couldn't have planned it any better, such synchronicity. Such divine guidance!

That morning, at the very last minute, I had changed the time for us to meet from 2:00 in the afternoon to 11:00 in the morning. We would probably have missed her had I not. Of all the people in the world to be sitting practically on top of us, here was this lovely, poised young girl, by herself, who overcame the anorexia that had plagued her. Meeting her meant the world to Lucia, a worried mom, who now held the hope that if this girl overcame it, her daughter could, too. The distressed look on her face softened to calm assurance.

We can communicate with our words

as well as our hearts, minds, and love.

TELEPATHIC CAT CALLS

I had just sold my apartment on the Upper East Side in New York City, where I raised my children, to seek a smaller, pied-à-terre-type place where I could do my healing work and writing. I found a place a few months later in the middle of winter and was already cohabitating on and off with my new husband of two years in his home in Connecticut. Our rescue cat, Jessi, resided in our Connecticut home alongside my own rescue dog, Shanti. We acquired Jessi from an animal shelter when she was a tiny kitten, and she came when we called her name, just like a dog. She was an inside cat, always within earshot, and probably learned early on that hearing her name meant treats were coming.

In the old apartment that I had not yet left, I was packing up some last-minute, sentimental treasures consisting of cards and various sundries my children made for me that were too precious to give to the movers. Those items from my children were my jewels—and I was the safety deposit box. In the midst of this one evening, my husband called to tell me, quite emotionally, that he couldn't find Jessi anywhere. He had searched everywhere and kept calling her name. He painfully admitted he had opened the door to get the mail and kept it open for a while. He wasn't paying attention, and she must have slipped out unnoticed. I wasn't going to be back in Connecticut for a few days, so I told him to leave some food and water on both the front porch and the back and to keep calling her name outside whenever he could. I tried to conceal my concern to keep him calm. I could sense the defeat in his tearful-sounding voice as if he believed she was gone forever. I was worried, too, because it was frigid outside—one night, it even fell below freezing. For some reason, though, I never gave up hope. I felt convinced that when I got home, we'd find her.

While still in the city, I wanted to try something I'd never done before: use my mind to connect with Jessi. Telepathically contacting a cat may sound crazy, but I wanted to try every avenue I thought possible. Oy—that could be a lot because I believe almost anything is possible. I focused on my cat and silently said, "I'll be back soon, Jessi. Go home. Jessi, go home." I repeated it over and over again, a few times a day, at the very least. Speaking to my husband each night, who sadly said she hadn't shown up, proved it was to no avail. But that didn't deter me from continuing to speak to her in my head or out loud. My gut told me we would find her once I got home.

Days later, when my husband came to pick me up along with my cherished boxes, we drove back to Connecticut in saddened silence. We arrived early that evening and left the warm car running while we brought my things into the house. Back in the car, we started down the driveway to search the neighborhood. I rolled down all the windows, turned the heat on high, and began yelling "Jessi" at the top of my lungs. And I can be loud. If she didn't hear me, I'm sure the entire neighborhood did! We spent over an hour that evening driving around while I stuck my head out the window calling for her until my throat was so sore and hoarse I could barely speak.

We finally gave up for the night, but I didn't give up silently telling Jessi to come home. Once inside, we grabbed a quick dinner of tuna sandwiches and hung out in the living room a bit. Then, my husband went upstairs to the bedroom for the night, but I wanted to try once more before settling in. I went out to the front porch, called for her, and waited a few minutes, hoping she would show up. Nothing. I did the same thing out the back door. Again, nothing. I was convinced she would magically appear when I came home, even after she'd been missing for over a week. I thought she could hear or feel me, that my voice would lead her home. But nothing.

I went upstairs in semi-defeat. After washing my face and brushing my teeth, something told me to give it one more try. Was it God? A higher power? The universe? My intuition? Who knows, but down the stairs I went. Again, I opened the front door, bundled myself up, went out onto the porch and yelled "Jessi" as loudly as I could a few more times, and waited. She didn't come. Then, on to the back porch, where I did the same thing and got the same disappointing result. Disheartened and defeated, I went back into the house, helped myself to a glass of water, and started up the stairs.

After a couple of steps, I thought I heard meowing. For a split second, I thought it might have been in my head since I was so anxious to hear it. But that didn't matter—I turned around and headed back down the stairs to try again. I opened the front door. Nothing. Then I heard the meowing, louder this time, and my dog, Shanti, sniffing loudly by the back door. I ran to open it, and there she was! Jessi, all perfectly dirty, the white parts of her coat now coated brown, and so thin, but so very healthy! I grabbed her and screamed with joy as I brought her into the house.

It felt like a miracle, an indoor cat outside for ten days in the frigid Northeast winter and not only surviving but coming home! Part of me always knew she would, even when the rest of me was heartbroken at the thought of never seeing her again. Did she assure me telepathically that she'd return? Is that why, deep in my heart, I never gave up? I'd bet a ton of treats she did.

PART VIII

NO RUSH

When we're in a place of stillness,

answers have room to surface.

Listen to your intuition—it's your

personal navigation system.

ANYBODY SEEN MY PURSE?

One day, my husband and I were holiday shopping at a large department store where the entire layout spread across one large, single floor. With so many sections to explore, we decided to split up to look for gifts for our kids—Bobby has three, and I have two. I meandered all over, from the shoe department and sock section (who doesn't need socks?) to toys and clothes. Suddenly, I stopped and froze. I didn't have my purse. It was a sage green, soft leather crossbody bag, not big, just a medium-sized pouch. I had everything in it: credit cards, driver's license, phone. Needless to say, I panicked. Stopping anyone I saw, I said, "I lost my purse! Did you see a sage-green shoulder bag?"

Next, I tracked down the store manager, told him what happened, and we both took up the search. At one point, I approached the shoe department again and saw a young girl with her mom. The ten-year-old immediately stopped trying on her sneakers, turned to her mom, and said, "Let's help her find her bag." *What a kind child*, I thought. My husband found us, and we five spread out in all directions like the fingers on an open hand.

After frantically running around to all the spots I thought I visited, I made a conscious decision to calm down and quiet my mind. Then something strange happened. Something, I don't know what, but *something* told me to go back to the scarf section, even though I had already checked there twice. I listened. I went back to check the scarfs, and there, right in front of me, hanging on a rack with other items, was my shoulder bag.

Elated, I retrieved the purse and searched out my detective team. After tracking them down and thanking everyone, I gave a special thank-you to the little girl. I then paid for my items, and we left the store.

I was not only grateful for listening to my intuition that day, but also for the reminder that when I'm open and allowing, giving myself a moment to slow down and listen, I free myself to experience things outside our so-called three-dimensional world, and endless outcomes become available. That's where the magic happens.

The universe speaks to all of us.

All we have to do is listen.

THERE IS ONLY ROOM
FOR LOVE

Many years ago, I was a cigarette smoker. I was also a bit of a yogi at the time. They definitely didn't go together, but there I was, puffing on my cig while on my way to sweating all that I'd just inhaled out of my body. I was a walking contradiction.

It was a balmy spring morning. Purple crocuses in the little gardens circling the trees by the curb finally added a splash of color to the city, and their blossoms overshadowed the small "Curb your dog" signs perched next to them. I set off for a lovely walk from my apartment to my yoga class on the Upper East Side. I really liked that studio. It was small, simple, down-to-earth, and inviting. No one seemed self-conscious, not even me, and I'm not a very limber person. I loved doing Vinyasa yoga. The movements flowed fluently from one pose to another with each breath.

It gave me a sense of calm and made me feel peaceful yet powerful. At least it usually did.

On this particular morning, as I entered the yoga shala, I felt a heavy weight bearing on my mind. I went through the motions but didn't feel fully present. My thoughts drifted, spiraled. I was happy when we finally went into the Savasana pose, also known as the corpse pose. With eyes closed, you lie on your back and allow your legs to sprawl freely with arms open at your sides, palms up. This time, though, while others around me were breathing deeply and calmly, I was wheezing. My smoker's lungs felt heavy, and I couldn't stop worrying about them.

My Savasana became overwhelmed with those thoughts that wouldn't stop—until they were interrupted by a strange woman's voice . . . in my head. *There is only room for love and friendship there.* I felt shocked to hear that voice in my head but at the same felt relieved by her words. The message's meaning came through loud and clear: there was no room in my lungs for smoke.

After the final pose and completion of the class, I threw on my hiking boots, grabbed my purse, and walked home. I haven't smoked since.

Sometimes, we have to view things

from another angle.

LIFE LESSONS FROM A KERATIN TREATMENT

Recently I had a natural version of a keratin hair treatment to gently tame the frizz but keep my curls. Although it took me many years to embrace my curls, I finally did, and I wanted to keep them. I was told not to wash my hair or get it wet for three days, or it would nullify the treatment's effects.

The next day, I ventured out to the grocery store. As usual, I parked far from the door to get those steps in. After checking out with my few items of arugula, avocado, and cucumber, I headed toward the door with my small bag of groceries. Uh oh. The parking lot pavement was wet. It was raining, and I had nothing to cover my head. So, what did I do? I ran like crazy to my car, pulled the driver's door open with great force, and tried to throw my body inside the SUV with equal heft. I didn't quite make it.

The upper point of the car door slammed right into my head, from the bottom of my eyebrow to about an inch above it. I slid over to settle into the rest of the car seat and pressed my sleeve tight against the open wound like I had learned in my wilderness first-aid class many years earlier. Home was just a half mile away, and fortunately, my husband had just arrived by the time I pulled up. He drove me to the emergency care center affiliated with the larger main hospital because it was much closer, smaller, and more comfortable. That's where I wanted to go.

After an almost two-hour wait, I was finally seen by a young physician's assistant named Adriana, who looked to be in her early thirties. She took one look at my wound and said she wasn't sure if she could do it because the cut was so deep into the muscle. She said I may need to go to the main hospital downtown. She later told me that the look on my face had made her change her mind. I don't know if I appeared terrified or determined or both, but in any case, this lovely young lady sewed me up. When I asked her how many stitches it would take, she said she didn't want to scare me and would tell me when she was done. A few minutes later, when she clipped off the last bit of thread, I asked, "Was it more than twenty?"

"No," she said. "It was nine." I felt relieved.

Then she said, "The stitches look like an 'L.'"

"Oh!" I said happily. "L is for love. I don't mind having an L for love on my forehead." I could tell she liked that remark because she responded with something nice. I don't recall her exact words, though. When she finally finished, I skipped out of there with my stitches and bandage on and thanked everyone.

When we got home, I called some family and friends to tell them what happened. They all said the same thing— "Why didn't you go to the main hospital and wait for a plastic surgeon? It's on your face!" I told them I was happy not to be sent there and that I really liked the woman who sewed me up. Plus, she was a Scorpio like me and had the same birthday as my dad. My dad had passed away twelve years earlier. What better sign than that?

Instead of being upset that I had to wait almost two hours and would have a scar on my face, I was thankful that it wasn't anything worse because the cut was very close to my eye. As I reflected on what happened to me that day, two things came to mind.

First, I felt I was given a message to slow down. Then, I saw the experience as an opportunity to understand that although I couldn't change what happened that day, I certainly knew I had a choice in how I chose to respond to it.

I chose to respond with L for love.

When we're still, we can hear the

music of our souls.

THE ROAD BEHIND
THE ROAD

None of it looked familiar. I felt I'd been hijacked into a world I didn't know. I was looking at the same semi-paved road that I had traveled every day for the past fifteen years with tall spruce forests on either side, which allowed only a glimmer of the sun to find its way through. Suddenly, it all seemed foreign. I recognized none of it. What was all so familiar to me became a landscape of the unknown. It was as if I looked at the palm of my hand, and my fortune had changed.

The scent of those tremendous trees, their secret whispers, embraced me in a way I had never experienced before. It awakened me, energized me. It seemed the wind aroused everything in its path, including me. Those are the moments, the ones that can't be described. The ones that reveal that there really is something so much bigger than us. We feel truly in the moment, and time stands still. As I leaned against my car door, the experience took my breath away, and tears flowed down my cheeks from the immersion of true joy that filled every cell of my body. I didn't move. I wanted it to last forever.

Sometimes life gets too noisy, and I lose sight of myself. Phones, computers, work, drama, the media, people's demands—everything feels hurried and distracts from the peace that revealed itself to me on that road. At least now I know I can return to the world of stillness where my soul speaks, and I can listen. Deep in my being, I know it is always there, waiting.

ACKNOWLEDGMENTS

I'd like to thank all those whose paths I was lucky enough to cross. You have gifted me with your presence. You added colors to my crayon box that didn't exist. You are the heart and soul of these vignettes, the magic. You—strangers, family, and friends—impacted me in the most profound ways.

To my parents, Audrey and Richard, for showing me the art of caring and everything else you taught me. You made me who I am today. To my daughter, Montana—this book would never have been written without you—and to my son, London, for always being there. I also would like to thank Danielle Joseph, my close friends (the Jericho girls and boy) for their well of love and support, and my husband, Bobby, for always listening and his unending reservoir of patience. A special thank-you to my wonderful editor Antonia Felix for her incredible insight, talent, and professionalism.

To Antonia Ka for her gentle guidance, Karen Gross for her unyielding encouragement, Hannah Zeltner for giving me a push start, Stephanie H. for believing in me and fueling my flame, Denise Cassino for helping me navigate this process, and a huge hug to my dog, Leaf, my constant writing companion who's always by my side.

To the universe—thank you for inviting me to *roam with you.* And to you, the reader, my deepest gratitude for taking the time to join me on this journey.

www.ingramcontent.com/pod-product-compliance
Lightning Source LLC
Chambersburg PA
CBHW031449160726
47994CB00005B/1953